QUICK SKILLS

ORGANIZING FOR SUCCESS

Holly Johnson
Career Solutions Training Group
Paoli, PA

VISIT US ON THE INTERNET
www.swep.com
www.thomson.com

SOUTH-WESTERN

TM

THOMSON LEARNING

Australia • Canada • Mexico • Singapore • Spain • United Kingdom • United States

SOUTH-WESTERN
THOMSON LEARNING™

Quick Skills: Organizing for Success
By Career Solutions Training Group

Vice President/Executive Publisher
Dave Shaut

Team Leader
Karen Schmohe

Project Manager
Laurie Wendell

Production Manager
Tricia Matthews Boies

Editor
Alan Biondi

Executive Marketing Manager
Carol Volz

Channel Manager
Nancy Long

Marketing Coordinator
Linda Kuper

Manufacturing Coordinator
Kevin Kluck

Cover Design
Tippy McIntosh

Copy Editor
Karen Davis

Compositor
Career Solutions Training Group

Printer
The Mazer Corporation

Betty Barrett
Instructor
Northern Kentucky Technical College
Covington, Kentucky

Dr. Barbara Buckbee
Career and Technical Education Director
Southwest Macomb Technical Education Consortium
Warren, Michigan

Kevin J. La Mountain
Dean of Career and Student Services
DeVry Institute of Technology
Phoenix, Arizona

Lyn O'Rourke
Career Services Director
The Academy of Professional Careers
La Mesa, California

Nicola Pidgeon
Coordinator of Business and Community Services
Schenectady County Community College
Schenectady, New York

Dr. Madelyn Schulman
Assistant Administrator
Office of School-to-Career Transition Services
New York City Board of Education
Brooklyn, New York

Doris Humphrey, Ph.D.: Project Manager
Jane Galli: Production Editor

13 East Central Avenue, Paoli, PA 19301
Telephone: 1-888-299-2784 • FAX: (610) 993-8249
E-mail: cstg@bellatlantic.net • Website: www.careersolutionsgroup.com

Explore these additional career resources from South-Western! Continue along the path to success with these flexible tools for job preparation and career enhancement!

Success Skills: Strategies for Study and Lifelong Learning, 2nd Edition

Success Skills equips users with the learning success strategies required in today's academic and workplace environments. With a focus on learning how to learn, thinking skills, communication skills, technology, and managing information, this book will develop key techniques necessary to achieve success in one's education and career.

ISBN: 0-538-72377-7

10-Hour Series

Become proficient in a variety of skills in a short amount of time. This series will enhance necessary business skills with little or no instructional intervention. The series also utilizes the Internet to bring users closer to today's technology for research and instruction.

E-mail in 10 Hours	ISBN: 0-538-69458-0
Getting Organized With Outlook	ISBN: 0-538-72385-8

SCANS 2000 Virtual Workplace Simulations

These CDs provide challenging, interactive workplace experiences that allow students to solve real-world problems and develop the skills most in demand by employers. As they complete the projects, students will analyze information, work in teams, and use critical thinking skills to make workplace decisions.

Making Complex Decisions	ISBN: 0-538-69823-3
Designing an Information System	ISBN: 0-538-69377-0

Personal Development for Life and Work, 8th Edition

Successful attitudes, interpersonal skills, critical thinking skills, and strong work ethics are qualities employers seek and reward. This updated edition is designed to help the new employee recognize the important role personal qualities play in the workplace. New features cover technology, diversity, ethics, and on-the-job problem solving.

ISBN: 0-538-69795-4

Working Smart, 2nd Edition

This text-workbook helps users learn how to be successful on the job by concentrating on dynamic job-keeping skills. Updated content covers current technologies, and hands-on exercises provide strategies for conquering the obstacles to success on the job.

ISBN: 0-538-69144-1

Join Us On the Internet
www.swep.com

SOUTH-WESTERN
★
THOMSON LEARNING

MAKING ORGANIZATION WORK FOR YOU

Alejandro Tavares, who oversees the inking department at Acme Comics, attended a weekend workshop about organizing. He learned many techniques for improving the way he plans and carries out his projects. For starters, he's already purchased a new telephone card file and calendar.

At morning break with his friend Remo, he says, "I never knew how much time I spent looking for lost papers and notes until I clocked myself today. I looked for one printer's business card for 15 minutes."

"So what did you do after you found the card?" asks Remo.

"Funny you should ask," Alejandro grins. "Even before I called the printer, I transferred all the information from her business card to my new telephone card file. When I needed to call back later, I went right to the spot where I filed the number."

Over the next several weeks, Alajandro continues to try some of the methods recommended at the workshop. One morning his supervisor, Mr. Mendel, calls him into the office and says, "Alejandro, we're growing so fast we need a better system to keep track of all the projects. I'd like you to coordinate the scheduling."

Alejandro is flattered that his organizing skills are appreciated. He tells Mr. Mendel, "I have lots of ideas, but for starters, I'll put up a large calendar. We can list on it all the projects, who's in charge of them, and when they are due."

"Sounds great," Mr. Mendel says. "It's a good thing you went to that seminar."

WORKSHOP 1

What's Inside

In these pages, you will learn to:

- identify your current organizing effectiveness.....p. 1
- use basic organizing strategies...........................p. 7
- choose the tools that can help you organize.............p. 13

Workshop 1: Making Organization Work for You

3

Workshop Introduction presents a short story relevant to the workshop.

What's Inside begins each lesson with clear learning outcomes.

Activities challenge learners to apply information from the workshops to real workplace situations.

ACTIVITY 2.1

What's Your Type?

Knowing your Type can help you become a better organizer. Review the material about personality preferences on page 20-21. Then write the letters from each pair that best describe your preferences. On the line labeled My Type, write the 4-letter abbreviation that identifies your preferences. Write a few sentences to show whether you agree or disagree that this is your Type and why.

My preferences

E or I _____

S or N _____

T or F _____

J or P _____

My Type: _____

_____
_____
_____
_____
_____
_____
_____
_____

A short assessment of your current organizing skills will help you identify the topics that need special attention as you go through the workshops. Complete the following assessment to see where you stand on important issues related to organizing. For each statement, check the response that best applies to you.

	True	False
1. There's only one way to organize, and once I've learned that I'm all set.	☐	☐
2. When I get a job, the company will tell me how to organize.	☐	☐
3. All companies use an alphabetic file system.	☐	☐
4. Organization takes up time better spent on other things.	☐	☐
5. People who aren't organized are lazy.	☐	☐
6. I should never throw out any business documents.	☐	☐
7. Electronic calendars always are better for organization than paper calendars.	☐	☐
8. Computers organize themselves automatically.	☐	☐
9. Everyone organizes in the same way.	☐	☐
10. Anyone with a disorganized desk is probably lazy.	☐	☐
11. Organizing doesn't take any special skill; it's just common sense.	☐	☐
12. Taking time to organize is a waste as long as you have a good memory.	☐	☐

All of these statements are untrue. If you already knew this, use this *Quick Skills* book to brush up on specific topics. If you answered "true" to any of the above questions, this book will help you become a more effective and productive organizer.

Self Check provides short self-assessment on the topic of organization.

To Do List

To Do
- ✓ Return phone calls
- ✓ Call Manuel
- ✓ Call Dr. Samson
- ✓ Prepare budget for the Caskill project
- ___ Print copy of client database and give to Sasha
- ___ Write summary of meeting with Marcus Langston
- ___ Develop a marketing letter to previous customers
- ___ Write survey questions for current customers
- ___ Fill out expense report

Information Boxes highlight interesting facts, findings, and trends in the area of organizing.

Organizing Your Space

✓ Write the addresses of new clients, vendors, and service providers in your address book as you receive them.

✓ Each time you set an appointment, schedule it on your calendar.

✓ Update changed telephone numbers, e-mail addresses, and web addresses as you learn of them.

✓ Keep only one calendar. Chances are you'll miss some appointments if you try to maintain more than one calendar.

✓ Staple business cards directly into your address book or in a telephone card file.

✓ Copy specific pages that will be needed for a business trip from your calendar or telephone file, so you don't have to carry a large, heavy portfolio.

GETTING CONNECTED

Many web sites give tips for getting motivated to stay organized. Try some of the following, remember to choose only the free areas of these site, avoid any web links that require payment:

http://www.frugalfun.com/officeorg.html

http://www.bizmove.com/business_tips/Smalltips13.htm

Getting Connected suggests web sites to visit for additional information on organizing.

Did You Know highlights interesting facts, findings, and trends in organizing.

?

Did you know

A recent article in *The Wall Street Journal* reported that the average U.S. executive loses six weeks per year retrieving misplaced information from messy desks and files!

" Good order is the foundation of all things "

—Edmund Burke
British statesman and philosopher

Quotations
Statements from authors, leaders, and celebrities add relevance, humor, and motivational messages.

WORKSHOP WRAP-UP

- Organizing cuts down on stress, helps you become more productive, and adds to your free time.
- Basic strategies for organizing include writing To Do lists, updating address books and calendars, keeping everything in its place, and maintaining a neat workspace.
- The tools needed for organizing vary from job to job.

Workshop Wrap-Up provides a recap of the key points from the workshop.

CONTENTS

This book is about the art of organizing. While "art" may seem an unusual description for something that is usually considered a skill, developing a system that helps you identify and store important papers, manage projects, and schedule your time takes creative thinking and decision making.

You can reach your goals sooner and with less frustration if you maintain a reasonable amount of order in your surroundings. Just being able to locate what you need when you need it is an important aspect of learning to organize.

Though organizing is an important skill, few people actually take a course that teaches them how to organize. To overcome that problem, in this *Quick Skills* book you'll learn concrete, specific guidelines for arranging your work area, your desk, and your files.

A major part of organizing is figuring out what you need to keep and what you need to throw away, how long to maintain records and where to store them, how to schedule your time, and how to keep track of projects. You'll learn all of this and more as you cover the material in the seven workshops on organizing.

♦ In Workshop 1, you'll discover how to make organization work for you, starting with the basics and ending with the tools you'll need.

♦ The relationship of personality to organization is covered in Workshop 2. There, you'll discover why it's easy for some people to organize and hard for others. You'll learn about your own personality and how it affects your organizational skills.

♦ Obstacles you'll face as you try to organize are covered in Workshop 3. These include such things as procrastination, interruptions, and delays.

♦ In Workshop 4, you'll learn techniques for maintaining a neat workspace and ways to create and manage a file system. Simple file rules for both an alphabetic and numeric filing system are provided.

♦ Strategies for managing your time and for coping with organizational setbacks are discussed in Workshop 5. The emphasis is on learning better ways to schedule.

♦ Project management, a key skill in today's work arena, takes center stage in Workshop 6. There, you'll learn why projects fail and how to manage several projects at once.

♦ Finally, Workshop 7 provides techniques for organizing your computer, including how and where to store documents and folders.

A short assessment of your current organizing skills will help you identify the topics that need special attention as you go through the workshops. Complete the following assessment to see where you stand on important issues related to organizing. For each statement, check the response that best applies to you.

	True	False
1. There's only one way to organize, and once I've learned that I'm all set.	❏	❏
2. When I get a job, the company will tell me how to organize.	❏	❏
3. All companies use an alphabetic file system.	❏	❏
4. Organization takes up time better spent on other things.	❏	❏
5. Everyone whose desk looks messy is disorganized.	❏	❏
6. I should never throw out any business documents.	❏	❏
7. Electronic calendars always are better for organization than paper calendars.	❏	❏
8. Computers organize themselves automatically.	❏	❏
9. Everyone organizes in the same way.	❏	❏
10. Anyone with a disorganized desk is probably lazy.	❏	❏
11. Organizing doesn't take any special skill; it's just common sense.	❏	❏
12. Taking time to organize is a waste as long as you have a good memory.	❏	❏

All of these statements are untrue. If you already knew this, use this *Quick Skills* book to brush up on specific topics. If you answered "true" to any of the above questions, this book will help you become a more effective and productive organizer.

Alejandro Tavares, who oversees the inking department at Acme Comics, attended a weekend workshop about organizing. He learned many techniques for improving the way he plans and carries out his projects. For starters, he's already purchased a new telephone number file and calendar.

At morning break with his friend Remo, he says, "I never knew how much time I spent looking for lost papers and notes until I clocked myself today. I looked for one printer's business card for 15 minutes."

"So what did you do after you found the card?" asks Remo.

"Funny you should ask," Alejandro grins. "Even before I called the printer, I transferred all the information from her business card to my new telephone number file. When I needed to call back later, I went right to the spot where I filed the number."

Over the next several weeks, Alajandro continues to try some of the methods recommended at the workshop. One morning his supervisor, Mr. Mendel, calls him into the office and says, "Alejandro, we're growing so fast we need a better system to organize and keep track of all the projects. I'd like you to coordinate the scheduling."

Alajandro is flattered that his organizing skills are appreciated. He tells Mr. Mendel, "I have lots of ideas, but for starters, I'll put up a large calendar. We can list on it all the projects, who's in charge of them, and when they are due."

"Sounds great," Mr. Mendel says. "It's a good thing you went to that seminar."

What's Inside

In these pages, you will learn to:

Why Organize?

Does juggling multiple projects complicate your life? Have you forgotten an important appointment, birthday, or anniversary lately? Do you promise yourself to get your papers under control after your next project is finished? If you answered yes to any of these questions, it's time to get organized. You'll get more pleasure out of each day if you eliminate the crises that come from being disorganized.

Think of organizing as a giant jigsaw puzzle. Fill in the borders of the puzzle with all the pieces that create the framework of your life, including projects, meetings at work, personal commitments, and recreational activities. Think of the inside of the puzzle as the connecting pieces—the tasks, schedules, and priorities that must fit together to form the complete picture. Once you organize the pieces and connect them correctly, you'll be able to meet your goals more effectively and efficiently.

Organizing Increases Productivity

Everyone gets disorganized at times, especially when under pressure. But some people stay chronically disorganized, which affects their productivity. Even simple organizational habits, such as filing and keeping an organized desk, can increase your sense of well being and your productivity.

People who can locate their important documents usually are well organized. They plan their schedules and maintain smart and efficient workspaces. They produce higher quality work, which leads to a more positive workplace experience for themselves and their employers. Employees who do not keep up with the organizational tasks of daily business may produce less work or experience greater stress.

Don't be deceived by the difference between the appearance of organization and the reality of organization. Some individuals appear organized but can't seem to prioritize effectively or meet deadlines. Others may be surrounded by clutter, yet have an organized way of thinking that keeps them on track. For instance, individuals whose personalities require visual stimulation need to *see* reminders of the projects they're working on. Their work spaces may appear cluttered, but they may be very effective at prioritizing and meeting schedules. In Workshop 2, you will learn how personality affects organization.

> " A place for everything and everything in its place. "
>
> — English Proverb

Stress Buster

Lack of organization can increase your stress at work. When you feel disorganized, do you bite your fingernails, twirl you hair, chew on a pencil, or engage in some other repetitive behavior? These behaviors are signs of stress. Doctors and psychologists say that an increasing number of employees suffer from chronic fatigue, depression, headaches, and other emotional and physical problems that may be caused by workplace stress. One cause of stress is feeling disorganized.

A few steps you can take to reduce organization-related stress at work are easy:

♦ Develop a practical system for filing your documents.
♦ Straighten papers.
♦ Arrange your work area for convenience.
♦ Prioritize projects.

A small amount of organizing can reduce long-term physical harm and bring additional harmony into your life.

Gaining Free Time

Part of being well organized is managing time efficiently. With good planning and scheduling, you'll create more free time for yourself. Because people work best when they take time to relax and re-energize their bodies, organizing your time for play and recreation can help you succeed at work.

Sasha Brek's company, a paper manufacturer in the northeast, gives employees a half-day off on Fridays during the summer as long as production quotas are met. It's a mystery to Sasha how 400 production workers can produce the same amount of paper when their work time is reduced by four hours. Why do you think this is possible?

Would you like to find extra hours just for yourself? Try the following ways to organize. While they may not result in a half-day off, following them will allow you to catch up on chores.

♦ Determine your objectives for the morning, day, or week.
♦ Establish a plan to achieve your objectives.
♦ Stick to your plan.

Did you know

A recent article in *The Wall Street Journal* reported that the average U.S. executive loses six weeks per year retrieving misplaced information from messy desks and files!

Organize...or Pay the Consequences

How does disorganization affect the workers described below? Place a check mark by as many answers as apply in each situation.

Marcella is an engineering student who has trouble organizing her materials. She often shows up to class late because her room is a mess and she can't find what she needs. What are the consequences of this disorganization?

_____She cannot write good papers.

_____She interrupts classes and frustrates her instructors.

_____She is not prepared.

_____She is tired most of the time.

Marco works as an assistant mechanic at an auto body shop. He is good with his hands, but he has a hard time organizing receipts for the work he's done. When it comes time to add up his earnings for his tax forms each year, he is not sure if he has all the documents he really needs. What is the consequence of this disorganization?

_____Marco has an ulcer.

_____Marco doesn't need to file his taxes.

_____Marco could be in trouble if his taxes get audited.

_____Marco pays more in taxes than he should.

Lorenzo works for a day care center. He is in charge of filing the permission forms that parents sign for their children to receive emergency medical treatment. Lorenzo is always behind in filing, and the important forms get mixed in with other papers. One day a little girl named Mailee breaks her arm on the playground. The parental consent papers are missing from her files. What is the result of this disorganization?

_____Mailee doesn't get the treatment she needs because the hospital will not admit her without parental consent.

_____Lorenzo's employer may fire him.

_____Mailee's parents may file a lawsuit against the day care center.

_____Lorenzo doesn't like his job.

Joel helps his mother with her catering business by keeping track of future jobs, including their locations, dates, and times. Twice in the last year he has gotten the dates of a wedding wrong and scheduled another event on the same weekend. His mother wants Joel to keep working with her because she feels he will become more responsible, but so far that doesn't seem to be happening. What are the consequences of Joel's disorganization?

_____Joel gets a job at a local greenhouse.

_____Joel's mother cannot afford to let him work for her.

_____Joel hurts the company's reputation.

_____Joel doesn't care about his mother.

Malik works as a project supervisor at an advertising agency. He likes his job, but he frequently misplaces drawings. To make deadlines, he often stays late to recreate his drawings. What could be the results of Malik's disorganization?

_____He is not seen as a good employee.

_____He may strain his personal relationships by working so much overtime.

_____He may get passed over for promotion.

_____Malik may develop stress-related health problems.

Start with the Basics

Don't panic if you aren't a perfect organizer. In the following section, you will learn basic organizing strategies. As you read, make a mental note of any strategies you can practice now or ones that you may want to start using.

Make a To Do List

Tying a string around your finger might have helped you remember your chores as a child, but in today's complex workplace, you'll need a comprehensive To Do list.

Some people prepare several To Do lists— for daily, weekly, and monthly tasks. As each task on the list is completed, it gets checked off. To Do tasks should be prioritized in the order they are to be completed, with the most important tasks being shown first.

No matter how comprehensive your To Do list is, you'll probably need

to add to it during the day. Leave blank space between items for this purpose.

Some people like to prepare their basic To Do list at the end of each afternoon, so they can start checking off items first thing each morning. Others prefer to create their list at the beginning of the day. Choose the method that works best for you and stick to it.

To Do List

To Do
- ✓ Return phone calls
- ✓ Call Manuel
- ✓ Call Dr. Samson
- ✓ Prepare budget for the Caskill project
- _____ Print copy of client database and give to Sasha
- _____ Write summary of meeting with Marcus Langston
- _____ Develop a marketing letter to previous customers
- _____ Write survey questions for current customers
- _____ Fill out expense report

> "You can ask me for anything you like, except time."
>
> —Napoleon Boneparte
> French Emperor

To Do, or Not to Do?

Make a list of five things you have to do today.

1. _____

2. _____

3. _____

4. _____

5. _____

Now prioritize the five items in order of importance. The most important items go first and the least important items go last.

1. _____

2. _____

3. _____

4. _____

5. _____

Return Calls Promptly

Answering messages should be one of your priorities each day. As you will receive some voice mail and e-mail messages when you are away from your desk, it's smart to set aside a specific time to answer the messages. By doing so, you can work several hours without interruption and also eliminate the danger of delaying important messages. With too much delay, old messages pile up or become lost.

First thing in the morning, right after lunch, and late in the afternoon are good times to return routine calls and e-mails.

Of course, client or customer calls are top priority and should be taken as received or returned as soon as possible.

Update Address Books and Calendars

Address books and calendars are great organizational tools, but they aren't helpful unless they're used correctly. A planner that contains an address and telephone section, a calendar, and other organizing tools can help the most unorganized person bring order to his or her work.

Several popular brands of address books, calendars, and planners are available. You can browse online office supply retailers to investigate the variety of desk organizers and accessories.

Write to Yourself

Posting notes where they will catch your attention is a good strategy to help you remember things. You can use Post It™ notes, which already have a sticky side, or make your own signs. Write in bold colorful letters and place the notes in eye-catching locations where they will get your attention. Some people like to stick notes to their computer monitor, on mirrors in their bathrooms, or on their doors, so they will see them first thing. Remind yourself of responsibilities such as deadlines, appointments, tasks to complete, and information you need to pass on to a coworker or client. When you have attended to the task written on a specific note, remove the note and throw it away.

Tidy Up

Hiding within stacks of papers, phone messages, CDs, floppy disks, and other clutter may be a few important notes waiting to be found. If your work area is cluttered, you may be surprised at what shows up when you start organizing. From filing drawers to desk tops, shops to offices, a neat workspace makes the job easier. Before you leave each day, take time to get your work area ready for the following morning.

- Put all documents and folders about the same subject together and file them in their designated space.
- Clean out your "in" and "out" box.
- Place pens, pencils, and paper clips in their designated place.
- Put unused supplies away.
- Arrange and stack printer paper.
- Close drawers and cabinet doors.

Organizing Your Space

✓ Write the addresses of new clients, vendors, and service providers in your address book as you receive them.

✓ Each time you make an appointment, schedule it on your calendar.

✓ Update changed telephone numbers, e-mail addresses, and web addresses as you learn of them.

✓ Keep only one calendar. Chances are you'll miss some appointments if you try to maintain more than one.

✓ Staple business cards directly into your address book or add the information to your telephone number file.

✓ Copy specific pages that will be needed for a business trip from your calendar or telephone file, so you don't have to carry a large, heavy portfolio.

Quick Skills

- Turn the page on your daily calendar.
- Leave your To Do list in the center of your desk.

Organize Books and Shelves

Do you take time to return books to their proper location on a shelf after each use, or do you stuff them in the first available space? Russ Weinfield, a computer programmer for a large agricultural company in Lincoln, Nebraska learned to properly reshelve books on a cold day in mid-January.

As Russ tells the story, his boss came to his cubicle and asked a question about a $1 million federal government proposal that the company had bound into a 428-page, hardback book. Not only could Russ not answer the question, he couldn't find the book on his shelves. His supervisor had to tell the government representative holding on the telephone line that he would call back later with the answer to the question.

Later, after searching for several minutes, Russ found the book in the corner of his office stacked under other books. He believes he damaged his standing with his supervisor by this one incident. Russ says that it provided the motivation he needed to arrange all his three-ringer binders and bound proposals by client name. Now, each time he uses a book, he makes sure he puts it back in its place.

Don't overlook your shelves when you organize. Alphabetize books and reference manuals by subject or author. After each use, return them to their correct order on the shelves. If your work requires large binders and reference manuals that take up a large amount of space, try to acquire shelves that accommodate these unusual size books.

Watch After Your Money

Tax records, accounts payable and accounts receivable records, and inventory lists should receive special attention. These documents are used for such simple purposes as proving expense account charges and for such complex purposes as defending the company in a dispute with the Internal Revenue Service. In the case of an IRS audit, they can make the difference in whether a company must pay large sums of money or none at all.

> **Make everything as simple as possible, but not simpler.**
> —Albert Einstein
> Mathematician

Financial papers should be organized separately from other documents and filed in a fireproof drawer or cabinet. A cardboard box won't do. File financial documents as soon as you finish with them.

Safeguard Computer Documents

Your computer needs to be organized too. As with paper files, computer documents should be labeled and stored in their proper place, or they should be deleted if they are no longer needed. This provides space in the computer's memory and allows it to operate more efficiently. Be sure to make back-up disks daily and store them in a secure and fireproof container. You'll learn more about organizing your computerized documents in Workshop 8.

ACTIVITY 1.3

Organizing Your Workspace

Make a list of ten routine tasks you complete each week. Write them in the left-hand column below. Then, in the right-hand column, write how you can organize these tasks for greater efficiency and time saving.

Weekly Routine Tasks   **Ways I Can Organize Better**

1. _____   _____

2 _____   _____

3. _____   _____

4. _____   _____

5. _____   _____

6. _____   _____

7. _____   _____

8. _____   _____

9. _____   _____

10. _____   _____

Quick Skills

Tools for Organization

For as many things that need organizing, there are as many tools and supplies for organizing them. The tools you use will depend upon the type of work you do. If you change jobs, you may need to change or update your tools. For example, a carpenter might use a pegboard to organize hand tools, a shed to store large equipment, and filing cabinets to house records. A travel agent might use a computer and special software to keep track of flight information, e-mail files to follow up e-customer requests, and a filing cabinet for brochures from resorts and hotels.

To think of it another way, imagine a person left a job as an accountant to become a teacher. For this person, the tools required for staying organized would change. He or she would no longer need tax filing computer software and a large filing system for important financial documents, but would need folders for students' work, pens for grading, and a calendar to schedule dates and times for meetings and parent-teacher conferences.

The best way to determine what tools you need for your job is to talk to people who have done the same type of work for a while and have a reputation for being well organized. Ask them what their techniques for organizing are and try those ideas first. Soon you will figure out what works best for you. Here are some common organizational tools and their uses.

? Did you know

An important part of organization is remembering things, especially important appointments, ideas, and facts. One odd, but proven, way to help yourself is to use one particular pen to write notes you will have to remember later.

Researchers conducted a series of studies in which students were asked to use the same pen to take tests as they used to write their notes and to study for the test. Students who always used the same pen were able to remember more and organize their thoughts better on the tests than the students who switched pens. The researchers concluded that the students associated the pen with certain information it had written.

This psychological trick may make it easier to recall times, dates, ideas, and facts when you are away from your desk or notes, simply by having your note-taking pen with you.

Pens, Pencils, and Paper

As a starter, you will need pens, pencils, and paper. You can find ones that you like for your type of work at any office supply store. You might want a broad-tip red pen to write yourself reminder notes, a fine-tip black one for signing important documents, and felt-tip markers for writing on presentation boards. Using tools that fit your job will improve your performance.

The Storage Tools

File folders and file cabinets often don't get the respect they deserve. Heavy-duty file cabinets, with locks if needed, provide a simple way to store your paper documents so they're easily accessible. If your files are incomplete or disorganized, you'll be at a disadvantage. With a well-functioning file system, important papers can be found quickly and efficiently.

♦ *Place related folders together in alphabetic order by topic or by name.* Client folders, for example, would be filed with the A's first, the B's next, and so on.

> ❝ Good order is the foundation of all things ❞
>
> —Edmund Burke
> British statesman
> and philosopher

♦ *Project folders should be identified by subject or title and filed alphabetically.* A dentist might maintain reference information filed under Bonding, Braces, Cavities, Root Canals, and other topics in ABC order.

♦ *Use colored labels on file folder tabs to separate major divisions or topics.* The teacher described in the preceding section might use blue tabs for freshman folders, yellow for sophomores, red for juniors, and green for seniors.

♦ *Use separate folders, drawers, or cabinets for dissimilar items.* Placing insurance and client files together is not a good match, but combining insurance and tax records in a drawer labeled Financial Materials is appropriate.

♦ *Make sure all file folders, drawers, and cabinets are labeled clearly.* Use as few words as possible on the label to clearly describe the contents.

♦ *Establish Active and Inactive drawers or cabinets.* When a file will not be used again, move it to the inactive section. Most physicians, for instance, move the folders of patients who have not been seen for five years to the inactive files.

Trash and Recycling Bins

Be relentless in throwing out anything in your workspace that is no longer needed. Discard advertisements and magazines that have no further value and rough drafts of any documents that have been updated. Give away computers and printers that are outdated and trash the things that don't work.

Clean tables, shelves, and drawers periodically before clutter accumulates. Getting rid of what you don't need makes it easier to find what you do need.

Hand-held Electronic Organizers

Hand-held electronic organizers are small computers that keep track of schedules, phone numbers, To Do lists, and appointments. They take time to learn how to use, and they aren't great for people who don't like gadgets. But many people find that they reduce the need for more than one calendar or address book because they store many types of information in a small, portable machine. They can even beep to remind you of an appointment.

Correcting Myths About Organization

Myth: Organizing Is Hard
Perhaps the most common misconception about organization is that it is difficult. In reality, organizing can be easy. You probably already have some organizational skills. By expanding them and making a commitment to organize a little each day, you will soon develop good organizational skills.

Myth: You Don't Need to Be Organized
Some people think they are organized enough to get along. They don't try to build their organizational skills. Allowing yourself to believe you can get along just fine without being organized is misleading.

Myth: Organizing Is Something You Buy, Not Something You Do
There are many tools you can buy to help you get organized, but the actual process of organizing is something you must do for yourself. You don't need every new electronic gadget that hits the market in order to be organized.

Myth: Organizing Cannot Be Learned
Some people feel like they will never be good organizers, but organization is a skill anyone can learn. Workers who are well organized were not born that way; they worked hard and learned good habits.

Planners and Calendars

Being organized means knowing where you are supposed to be when. Planning books and calendars have the same basic function, but they lay out the times and spaces in different ways. You may choose to use either a planner or a calendar, or you may use a combination of the two to plan your time effectively. These tools are more familiar to most people than hand-held organizers, but they are used for the same purposes, and they are useful for people who don't like electronic devices.

ACTIVITY 1.4

The Right Tools for You

Think about your current job or one you would like to have. List the tools that will help you organize efficiently. Then, describe why each tool is needed in your work.

Tools I Need for Organizing

_____

_____

_____

_____

_____

_____

_____

_____

Why I Need This Tool

_____

_____

_____

_____

_____

_____

_____

_____

GETTING CONNECTED

Many web sites give tips for getting motivated to stay organized. Try some of the following, remember to choose only the free areas of these sites, avoid any web links that require payment:

http://www.frugalfun.com/officeorg.html

http://www.bizmove.com/business_tips/Smalltips13.htm

To review desk organizers and accessories online, try these sites:

http://www.staples.com

http://www.officedepot.com

WORKSHOP WRAP-UP

- Organizing cuts down on stress, helps you become more productive, and adds to your free time.
- Basic strategies for organizing include writing To Do lists, updating address books and calendars, keeping everything in its place, and maintaining a neat workspace.
- The tools needed for organizing vary from job to job.
- Organizing is a learned skill.

PERSONALITY AND ORGANIZATION

2 WORKSHOP

onstantine has been working as a freelance graphic designer for the past five years. Recently he took a position on a design team for a local university. As with many new employees, he wonders whether he will be compatible with his coworkers. Already, he's noticed that most of the desks are organized and neat—one person puts every file folder away before he picks up another.

Constantine needs stacks of materials laid out on a table to remind him of the work to be done. "Out of sight, out of mind," is his usual style. People have teased him about not being able to see the top of his desk. While his type of organizing hasn't kept him from performing efficiently in the past, he's never been part of such a structured group before.

His new boss, Angie McAlree asked him to take a personality test before he started work. At first, Constantine wondered if the test would show that his creative personality was connected to disorganization. Fortunately, Angie understands. She explained that people with different personality types organize in different ways.

She said she recognizes that his personality requires visual cues. That makes a lot of sense to Constantine, since he likes to organize his project folders and disks by color.

One day Angie suggests that Constantine order several low shelves for his office so he can arrange all his stacks. The result is amazing. Constantine's office looks less cluttered, and he's able to walk to a shelf and review his drawings.

What's Inside

Relating Personality to Organization

Knowing your personality type can help you understand why you organize (or don't organize) your work in a particular way. Do you jumble your papers together on your desk or store each one neatly after finishing with it? Do you cover all available desktops with your papers? Have you ever wondered why?

Different personalities favor different organizational techniques. In some ways, your desk reflects your personality. Maybe it's the neatest one in the office, or maybe it's the messiest. What's important is to find the type of order that's best for you—a system that makes you efficient. For most of us, a moderate degree of neatness helps.

Chances are that if your desk is always neat and clear of miscellaneous papers you also keep a tidy bedroom, store your socks and underwear in separate drawers, and are on time or early for appointments. Organizing should be easy for you because your personality likes order.

Your best friend, on the other hand, may be chronically late for appointments, cover every desktop available with miscellaneous papers, and never seem to worry about it. Your friend's personality doesn't have your sense of order. To him or her, a file stored in a drawer is "out of sight, out of mind." What is "mess" to one person may be "order" to another.

The smartest, most creative person in your workplace may have the cleanest—or messiest—work area. It's smart to strive to understand your own and your coworkers' personalities and use this knowledge to become more productive. What's important is that your organizational style is efficient, that the system works for you.

Connecting Personality and Organization

- ◆ Each individual has a personal way of organizing.
- ◆ Understanding your organizing style is the first step toward working efficiently.
- ◆ You can learn techniques for working with people whose organizational style is different from yours.

Personality Indicators

Several personality assessments can be used to help you learn about yourself and others. Two that have been extensively researched and used worldwide are the Myers-Briggs Type Indicator® (MBTI) and the Keirsey Temperament Sorter. Based on the work of psychologist Carl Jung, they measure personality types on four scales: (1) whether you get your energy from yourself or from being with others, (2) how you gather information, (3) how you make decisions, and (4) how much structure you prefer to have in your daily life.

Start measuring your Myers-Briggs personality Type by answering several questions. When you finish, your answers will lead you to identify yourself by one letter from each of four pairs of letters—E or I, S or N, T or F, J or P. This is a very simplified and abbreviated version of the personality Types. To confirm your Type you would need to go through a more extensive test administered by a certified individual.

1. Does working with others energize or tire you? Do you relish quiet time or try to fill it with actions?

    People whose energy comes from contact with others are identified as extroverts (E), while people who get their energy from quiet time alone are identified as introverts (I).

2. Do you gather information primarily by using your senses of sight, sound, touch, taste, and smell or do you prefer to use your intuition (your sixth sense) to understand what is around you?

    If you depend on the senses, you are most likely a sensing (S) type, or if you use intuition, you're probably an intuitive (N) type.

3. Do you form conclusions and make decisions by thinking things through rationally or do you trust your hunches and feelings?

    People who are more comfortable with facts and logic are considered the thinking (T) type, while those who are more concerned about feelings are identified as the feeling (F) type.

4. Do you prefer to order your life in a structured manner or in a flexible, spontaneous way?

    Individuals whose preference is for order and schedules are known as the judging (J) type, and those who prefer flexibility and spontaneity are considered the perceiving (P) type.

Everyone possesses all eight of the preferences to varying degrees. But when you have the opportunity to choose, you tend to favor one of the preferences in each pair. Review the information in the box on page 21 for additional information about preferences.

The personality instruments actually go one step further. They produce a 4-letter personality Type developed from the descriptions in Nos. 1-4 above. For example if in No. 1, your energy comes from contact with others, the letter that identifies your Type of personality is probably (E). If you decided in No. 2 that

Myers-Briggs Type Indicator and MBTI are registered trademarks of Consulting Psychologists Press, Inc.

you prefer to make decisions based on your Intuition, the letter N probably identifies you. After you identify the letters in Nos. 3 and 4 that most accurately describe your preferences, you can put them together for a 4-letter combination.

Everyone possesses all the characteristics identified by each letter some of the time. But the characteristics that are strongest are called preferences. They provide a personality description based on your combination of preferences.

If your personality type is ENTP, you might be described as someone who feels energized by having a lot of things going on, is a creative problem solver, makes decisions logically, and is open to new ideas and possibilities. If you are an ISFP, you might be described as someone who feels energized by spending time alone in contemplation, prefers dealing with the present over thinking about possibilities, is a supportive team member, and makes spontaneous decisions.

What It Means to Have Your Personality Type

Once you know the letter abbreviations of your personality type, you will want to know what they mean. The chart below describes some of the characteristics of each personality type.

Personality Preference	Common Qualities of Personality Types
Introverted type	inner directed; thinks before acting; wants private time to analyze information
Extroverted type	outer directed; acts and then thinks; social; likes to talk about things to before making decisions
Sensing type	focuses on the present, sees what is; wants practical applications; communicates directly; wonders how we can use what we have
Intuitive type	focuses on the future, sees what might be; communicates in more creative ways; wants to talk about possibilities; wonders how we can change things for the better
Thinking type	values objective analysis; logical; has a long-term view; wants facts and figures
Feeling type	values personal relationships; interested in what effect ideas will have on people; subjective, personal, immediate view
Judging type	makes decisions about what to do, when to do it, and so on; likes to know where he or she stands
Perceiving type	keeps options open; spontaneous and flexible; discovers life as he or she goes along

As this is only a brief explanation of the MBTI, you should study the Types further. Many books on the subject of Type are available at your local bookstore and from on-line sources.

ACTIVITY 2.1

What's Your Type?

Knowing your Type can help you become a better organizer. Review the material about personality preferences on pages 20-21. Then list the letters that best describe each of your preferences and write a brief description of the preference. On the line labeled My Type, write the 4-letter abbreviation that identifies your preferences. Discuss in a few sentences whether you agree or disagree that this is your Type and why.

My preference   Description of preference

E or I _____   _____

S or N_____   _____

T or F_____   _____

J or P _____   _____

My Type: _____

_____

_____

_____

_____

_____

_____

_____

_____

_____

_____

_____

_____

Temperament Labels

Clinical psychologist and best-selling author Dr. David W. Keirsey developed Temperament labels and descriptions for different personalities. Known as Guardians, Artisans, Idealists, and Rationals, the Temperaments provide a fuller understanding of the relationship of personality to life and work habits, such as organizing. For a more in-depth discussion of Dr. Keirsey's Temperament, refer to his book *Please Understand Me II* or the web site listed on page 30.

While categorizing a person's work habits narrowly according to Temperament would be inappropriate, you can learn general information that may be helpful. The discussion that follows will provide glimpses of how some people of different Temperaments might relate to organizing.

Guardians

ESTJ, ISTJ, ESFJ, ISFJ

Most Guardians are good at logistics, scheduling, and planning, but some may not always follow through on plans. This has to do with their tendency to take on too many things at once. Sometimes, Guardians can't say "no" when asked to volunteer. Guardians usually have a great deal to organize because of their broad interests.

Artisans

ESTP, ISTP, ESFP, ISFP

Being spontaneous, Artisans are very creative. They find unique ways to express themselves. They love to improvise. Artisans may be easily frustrated by structure and rules that don't work, and they may find organization tiresome and difficult. Nevertheless, if they can't find the supplies, tools, and documents they need, they can become frustrated.

Idealists

ENFJ, INFJ, ENFP, INFP

Idealists are the dreamers, the people who visualize all the possibilities in life. Sometimes people don't understand them because they often communicate abstractly and tend to focus on final goals. This can distract them from the here and now, the details. Since organization depends on staying focused at most times; some, but not all, Idealists may have trouble caring about organizing.

Rationals

ENTJ, INTJ, ENTP, INTP

Rationals are extremely good at organization. It seems to come naturally to them. They think problems through logically, and solve them rationally after considering the possibilities. Some Rationals may have difficulty relating to people who are unorganized. This can become an organizational problem of its own, especially if Rationals are unable to work well with others on collaborative projects.

Please Understand Me II by David W Keirsey, Prometheus Nemesis Books, May 1998.

Easy... Difficult?

From what you have learned about your personality Type, analyze whether organization will be easy or difficult for you, then place a check mark in the correct blank. Describe any organizational problems you may encounter because of your personality Type.

My personality type indicates that organization will be _____easy _____difficult for me.

My personality type may affect my ability to organize because: _____

_____

_____

_____

_____

_____

_____

Avoiding Personality Pitfalls

By being aware of your Temperament, you can compensate for deficiencies that may affect your ability to organize. Read the following descriptions of organizing pitfalls typically experienced by different personalities and develop strategies for overcoming them.

Guardians

Though Guardians are good organizers generally, they can become overextended. If you are a Guardian, limit the number of projects you accept at one time. A good rule of thumb is to reduce by one or two the number of projects you think you can accept at once. Remind yourself that you won't be able to follow through if you take on too much.

Artisans

Artisans are gifted with the ability to bring fresh ideas and perspective to a work group. They tend to be determined and persistent in pursuing the things they enjoy, but organizing may not be one of their pleasures. Artisans benefit from reminding themselves why organizing is important. If you are an Artisan, you probably respond to sensory stimuli. Try posting brightly colored organizational reminders or inspirational quotes about organizing around your workspace. Artisans tire quickly when it comes to organizing, so taking mini-breaks is a useful strategy for breaking up tasks.

Reminder: Project Due April 12

Idealists

Some Idealists have trouble staying focused on a task because they get caught up in ideas, goals, and plans for the future. Their desks may be covered with stacks of paper about a variety of topics arranged in no particular order. What seems to help them is anything that keeps their minds from wandering. If you are an Idealist, listening to music while you organize may motivate you, or you may prefer to get things done at odd times of day when the office is quiet and you won't get distracted. Having a friend check up on you to see how far along you are in an organizational task may also be helpful.

Rationals

Because Rationals are good at staying organized, they sometimes have a hard time imagining how difficult it can be for others. This can create friction among team members, and, ultimately, make it hard for Rationals to put their talents for organizing to work. If you are a Rational, it may be helpful to remember that organization does not come naturally to everyone. Rationals sometimes get impatient with people who don't keep things orderly. If you are a Rational, share your effective organizational methods with your coworkers. If you take an instructive role, you may become more tolerant and patient with others.

ACTIVITY 2.3

A Few Strategies, Just for Me

Your manner of thinking and organizing is individual. Once you recognize your organizing strengths and weaknesses, develop strategies to keep yourself organized. Check the items below that you believe will assist your personality Type in becoming a better organizer, then write a few other ideas that might help you stay organized.

_____ I should use visual reminders, especially bright colors.

_____ Learning to say "No" would help.

_____ I should respect the idea of organizing more.

_____ Taking breaks during organizing is essential.

_____ I should work alone; otherwise I'll get distracted.

_____ It helps me to have someone check on my progress when I work.

_____ I get distracted very easily, so I should minimize my distractions while organizing.

_____ Practicing patience with poor organizers should be a goal for me.

Other ideas to keep me organized:

1._____

2._____

3._____

Evaluating Coworkers' Personalities

Observe your coworkers at their jobs and ask a few tactful questions to help you identify their personality Type. You may be able to find ways to support their organizational preferences and cut down on misunderstandings that may occur because of your differences. Try some of the recommendations below for maintaining harmony with individuals of each personality Type.

Guardians

Your colleague's desk is neat as a pin, but she seems so busy you're concerned about interrupting her for a document you need. This person may be a Guardian Type, someone who is generally organized, but who takes on too much at once. Before you begin working on a project with her, establish what you will need at different stages of the project and ask for these in advance. Schedule meeting dates and times so she can write them on her calendar. By asking your important questions up front, you will not interfere with your coworker's busy schedule and you'll be able to do your part of the project. Here are some other tips:

♦ Learn what other projects the person is working on so you have a better sense of her time commitments.

♦ Complete your own tasks well in advance of any deadline.

Artisans

Being chronically disorganized, forgetting what you ask them to do, and getting caught up in the creative side of things are characteristics Artisans have difficulty overcoming. Because they respond well to sensory stimuli, write bright reminder notes to Artisans, give them information in a unique folder, or leave a creative voice message that stimulates them to remember. Other tips you may want to try are:

♦ Think of creative ways to inspire your coworkers to do tasks you need them to do.

♦ Check up on their progress.

♦ Share a stimulus-evoking reward after the task is complete (a treat, a flower, a compliment).

Idealists

Working with Idealists may be challenging because of their lack of structure. Try these strategies:

♦ At the start of a conversation, a task, or a project, identify the goals. Say, "I need to ask you a question about the meeting we're having on February 19 to discuss the Marshall project. What would you like me to cover in the presentation?"

> " The meeting of two personalities is like the contact of two chemical substances: if there is any reaction, both are transformed. "
>
> —Carl Jung
> Famous psychologist

- Return to the subject if your coworker gets off the topic. Say, "Let's set a time to talk about the DeSimone project. For now, will you give me a few more ideas about the meeting on the 26th?"
- By helping an Idealist stay focused, you can guide the collaborative activity. Provide frequent reminders of what you need from the Idealist and give positive feedback when the two of you meet your goals.

Rationals

Ask Rationals, whose neatness and organization can be compulsive, to share their tricks of the trade. They'll be happy to help you with your bad habits. Your reaching out to them will enhance their cooperation.

Keeping Personalities in Perspective

Knowledge of personality Types helps individuals develop tolerance for others, but it can have drawbacks. Scott Arbuthnot, a corporate training designer from Australia, cautions against using information about personality Types to pigeonhole and judge people. He reminds us that all personality Types are equally valid and notes that we are all capable of operating "outside our preferences or comfort zones" when needed. It just takes a little work.

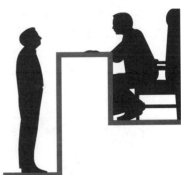

Coping with Someone Who Is Chronically Disorganized

Here are some ways to keep yourself on track when you work with someone who is chronically disorganized:

- Stay focused on your priorities. Don't get blown off course.
- Make copies of important documents if you think a coworker might lose them.
- If you need to exchange materials, try delivering them in a neon or brightly colored folder that will be harder for the coworker to misplace.
- If you think your coworker simply doesn't know any organizational strategies, you may try sharing some of your own. Be tactful—this can backfire.

Workshop 2: Personality and Organization

Organization and Stress

A certain amount of stress is normal and even productive in every day business, but if stress becomes excessive, good organizational habits can be hard to maintain. Workers have two primary organizational reactions to extreme stress. Either they become hyper-organized or their organizational habits fall apart completely.

Guardian and Rational Types tend to become hyper-organized, while Artisans and Idealists may become disorganized. Hyper-organization, which sounds good at first, is as much a problem as disorganization. Both behaviors lower efficiency and waste time.

Hyper-organized individuals spend time organizing things that do not need to be organized. They may compulsively separate paper clips by color, frequently sharpen pencils to perfect points, or fiercely note and file every conversation.

Whichever your personality Type, you will occasionally be faced with stress related to organizing. Following these guidelines will help:

♦ Let someone, a colleague or supervisor, know right away that you need time to get organized.
♦ Take mental vacations. You don't have to leave your office—just allow yourself a few moments each day to focus on something outside work that calms or motivates you.
♦ Don't be a hero. Allow people to help you organize and ask for help when you need it.

> **The better work people do is always done under stress.**
>
> —William Carlos Williams
> Doctor, Poet, and Author

Complimenting Other Organizational Styles

Staying organized amid confusion or chaos is challenging, but in today's fast-paced workplace, you often have no choice. Setting good organization as one of your top priorities will help you maintain the focus you need. You might try listing "Organize" at the top of each day's To Do list. Here are a few other helpful hints:

♦ Keep the lines of communication open with all your coworkers.
♦ Establish and stick to a schedule.
♦ Ignore others' personality traits that bother you.
♦ Post reminders to help you meet deadlines.
♦ Let people know what keeps you focused.
♦ Support individuals whose personalities and organizing styles are different from yours.

Quick Skills

Accommodating the Organizational Preferences of Others

It's time to apply what you've learned about the relationship of personality preferences to organizing. Answer the questions below about a coworker and make recommendations for accommodating his or her organizing style.

1. Write the name of a colleague whose organizational habits are different from yours.

    _____

2. What is this person's probable personality Type?

    _____

3. Which behaviors does the person exhibit to suggest this personality Type?

    _____

    _____

4. Describe a problem you have had with the person in the past that might be related to different organizing or structuring habits.

    _____

    _____

5. Write what you could do differently in the future to work with this person.

    _____

    _____

Now, examine your own personality and experiences with stress and answer the following questions.

1. What stresses me?

    _____

2. How does stress affect my ability to stay organized?

    _____

3. What do I usually do to help myself get out of or avoid stressful situations?

    _____

4. What could I do in the future to keep organized even when I'm stressed?

    _____

GETTING CONNECTED

For more information about your personality Type, try the following links:

http://frontier.dreamhost.com/askmyers.htm

http://www.keirsey.com

http://www.mbtypeguide.com/Type/types.html

WORKSHOP WRAP-UP

- People with different personalities organize differently.
- David Keirsey named the Myers-Briggs Types: Guardians, Artisans, Idealists, and Rationals.
- It is easier to stay organized when you know what Type of personality you have.
- You can reduce conflicts when you understand your coworkers' personality preferences.
- Whatever your personality Type, you will occasionally face organizing-related stress.

Quick Skills

Ozilline Black works for an Internet start-up company that provides users with reference materials on the Web. Today she is trying to organize a section of the site on Asian history that she will present in a staff meeting tomorrow. Like every other day, progress is slow.

Although she's been at the office since 7:00 a.m. and it's now lunch time, she's still answering voice mails and trying to organize some of the piles of papers on her desk. As she watches her colleagues come and go in the hall, she becomes distracted and loses concentration. She decides to take a break to get a soda. Since her best friend's office is right by the soda machine, she stays to chat for a few minutes.

After Ozilline returns, her coworker Sashi stops in to discuss an idea he's working on. Just as Ozilline is about to start on her project again, she gets a personal phone call. In late afternoon, Greg, Lola, and Mahandi interrupt her to ask questions.

When her supervisor stops to check on the Asian history project at 4:30, Ozilline tells him she will be working late again, and he expresses disapproval about having to pay overtime. Although Ozilline explains that it's been a busy day, she knows she's been disorganized, jumping from one task to another and delaying small, uninteresting parts of the Asian project. She vows that tomorrow she will get everything done on time.

Eliminate the Obstacles

Obstacles, both self-imposed and from external sources, often interfere with good organization. Three obstacles you should reduce or eliminate when attempting to organize are procrastination, interruptions, and delays. Any of these combined with other bad habits reduces your effectiveness.

Procrastination

Procrastination occurs when you put off something you know should be done now and get involved in another activity that is less important, but more interesting or more fun. Often, people procrastinate because they're disorganized. It just seems too hard to get started when supplies, tools, directions, folders, and other items needed for a job are out of order, lost in stacks, or bunched together in a drawer.

Procrastination affects companies in many ways. A few of the more glaring ones are described below.

Failure to meet a deadline

People often put off organizing a project because it seems too large, too complex, or too uninteresting. Delaying may reduce your ability to finish the project on time.

> " If the person who did the job before me had been organized, I would never have learned all the ins and outs of my job. "
>
> —Patti Dickerson
> Entrepreneur

Inability to provide a quality product

Procrastinating at the beginning of a project may mean you'll have to rush at the end. This often leads to poorly developed ideas or poor quality workmanship.

Loss of motivation

Motivation takes a nose dive when you procrastinate. It's human nature to lose interest and enthusiasm when a project drags on and on.

Wasting the employer's resources

An employer loses money when workers procrastinate. By continuing to pay wages while receiving little benefit from the workers' time, a company becomes less productive and profits suffer.

Loss of personal time

On a personal note, procrastinators often end up staying late at the office. When they'd rather be relaxing at home, they are still trying to catch up on their work from earlier in the day.

Correcting the Problem

To break the cycle of poor organization caused by procrastination, follow these guidelines:

1. **Make organizing a top priority.**
   Just like becoming a better sports player, winning a debate, or doing anything else that's important, organizing must be one of your top priorities if you want to be successful at it. If one of your goals is to maintain good fitness, you probably visit the gym several times a week to train. Similarly, if one of your goals is to be well organized, you'll need to set time aside to train.

2. **Allow time for completion.**
   Start each day by deciding what work needs to be accomplished during the day, then allot an estimated amount of time to complete each task. Make sure you are realistic about what you can accomplish in one day, and don't overload yourself.

3. **Break big jobs down.**
   Sometimes the complexity of a job is overwhelming. If you know that a task will take about six hours to finish, break the job into parts and allot ample time to complete each part.

4. **Create a checklist.**
   Make a list of the tasks for which you allotted time. As you finish each task, place a check mark by the entry. If you stick to your plan for the day, you will gain a feeling of accomplishment each time you cross an item off the list.

5. **Sort and store.**
   Set aside time each day to sort and store supplies, tools, documents, and files in a handy place so they will be readily available the next time you want to use them. For example, if you take the time to put your reference books back on the bookshelf in proper alphabetical order after you use them, they'll be easy to find later.

A Few Simple Rules

Concentrate on easy ways to stay organized. You can begin by using some of the successful techniques of highly organized people.

✓ Analyze each task before getting started so you know exactly what items you need and how they should be organized.
✓ Leave on your desk or in your workspace only the items you need for the current task.
✓ Put away supplies and materials you no longer need before adding new ones to your desk.
✓ Clear your workspace at the end of the day.

Think how much faster this small bit of organization is compared to searching through stacks of books on tables, the floor, or a window sill just to find the right one.

6. **Avoid distractions.**
Do you read your e-mail several times a day, receive and make personal phone calls often, listen in on conversations, and comment on what coworkers are saying without being asked? If so, you distract yourself and others and you waste your employer's time and money.

One method of avoiding distractions is to arrive at the office early or stay late so that fewer things interrupt your work. Don't let your natural instinct to chat and be friendly cause you to be viewed negatively by other workers who want to finish their work and go home as soon as possible at the end of each day.

7. **Stop only for short breaks.**
Once you get going on your work, stop only for short periods so you won't lose your momentum. If you stop for too long, you may become involved in another activity and find it hard to get started again.

8. **Invite others to your work area.**
Do you clean your room, apartment, or home when you're expecting a guest? If the answer is yes, then try inviting a coworker or client to visit your workspace. You may become motivated to organize and arrange your area if you know visitors will see it.

9. **Organize a little each day.**
Most employers require you to leave your workspace at least moderately tidy at the end of each week. If you organize a little each day, your organizing task at the end of the week will be minor. Chances are you don't want to spend Friday afternoon throwing away clutter that you've allowed to accumulate all week.

10. **Fight fatigue and temptation.**
When you are busy or tired, it's tempting to leave materials, files, supplies, and tools where you used them last. Instead, take the time to put away everything that won't be needed when you start your next task. Wash out drink cups, put reports in binders, and store tools and materials where they go. Return magazines, books, samples, and other papers to their owners or to the proper file.

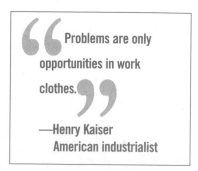

"Problems are only opportunities in work clothes."

—Henry Kaiser
American industrialist

11. Suppress the compulsion to over organize.

Surprising as it may sound, some people over organize. These compulsive organizers put all the red pencils in one container, the blue ones in another, and the ball point pens in yet another. It's possible to go overboard. You won't have time to work if you organize your day away.

A Few Tricks

For many procrastinators, the hardest part of getting organized is beginning. Here are some ways to motivate yourself to start:

◆ **Get Started**

Do anything you can to get the ball rolling. Trick yourself if necessary. Like a swimmer about to jump into cold water, you may want to hold back from organizing. Ultimately, you have to find some way to take the plunge. One way competitive athletes encourage themselves to begin a race is to remember that their bodies will adjust to the pace once they get started. You can get started on your organizing by reminding yourself that you will develop momentum once you get started.

◆ **Find a Partner**

No rule says you have to organize by yourself. Some people, especially people who gather energy from interacting with others, find organizing easier when they work with a partner. You can help your coworker organize his or her projects, then he or she can help you organize yours. Just be sure not to get distracted by talking.

◆ **Reward Yourself**

After a big organizing project, take some time out to do an activity that is fun.

Did you know

Did you know that the average *Fortune* 1000 worker receives 83 messages a day? According to a USA Today/Gallup poll, 84 percent of surveyed workers say they are interrupted three or more times an hour by the telephone, e-mail, faxes, notes, phone message slips, or pagers.

Type of Interruption	Per Day	Type of Interruption	Per Day
Regular phone messages	32	"Post-it" notes	6
E-mail messages	14	Telephone message slips	5
Voice mail messages	11	Pager messages	4
FAX documents	9	Cellular phone messages	2

ACTIVITY 3.1

Stop Procrastinating

Read the following anecdotes, then circle P if the person is procrastinating or O if the person is staying organized. If you answer P, provide suggestions about how to eliminate the problem. If you answer O, describe a nice reward for the person.

1. Angelina is creating a system for filing information about her local clients. She stops to eat lunch then goes back to her task.   P   O

   Recommendation or Reward: _____

   _____

2. Marlow comes into work early to organize his computer files by deleting ones he doesn't need any longer. He allows himself to play a game or two of computer solitaire before getting to work.   P   O

   Recommendation or Reward: _____

   _____

3. Mara stops making up a list of what she has to do today and goes to the water fountain, where she stops to talk to some friends.   P   O

   Recommendation or Reward: _____

   _____

4. Pramish answers her voice mail, returns two business calls, then calls her best friend to set a time to get together after work.   P   O

   Recommendation or Reward: _____

   _____

5. Logan organizes the papers on his desk by throwing things away, but when he comes across a report his son Denny wrote, he takes it around the office and shows it to everyone.   P   O

   Recommendation or Reward: _____

   _____

6. Roger and Oleg are working together to clean out Oleg's old files; they stop for a while to talk about a mutual friend who used to work in their office.   P   O

   Recommendation or Reward: _____

   _____

Quick Skills

Interruptions

Organization is a process, and it's easy to lose track of what you were working on when you are stopped by an interruption. Say you're developing ideas for a report and keying them into the computer when the telephone rings. Getting your thought pattern back after you finish the phone call can be challenging. You may lose a valuable idea and not be able to recover it.

Unfortunately, some interruptions are unavoidable. For many who work with customers and suppliers, interruptions are part of their job. They deal with concerns, answer questions, troubleshoot, and respond to crises.

Researchers at the Gartner Group report that by 2002 most jobs in most U.S. industries will be devoted to responding to issues, opportunities, and problems, rather than to doing specific tasks. Basically, people will be interrupted frequently and will have to find ways to keep themselves organized in spite of the interruptions.

The effect that getting interrupted has on organizing can't be fixed by simply changing your own habits, since the interruptions are caused by other people. There are ways, however, to cut back on constant, or unproductive interruptions so you have a better chance of working in an organized manner.

How to Avoid Interruptions

You can control certain factors that contribute to interruptions. Try some of the suggestions given below:

♦ *Set up your workspace to minimize interruptions.* Do you know you can actually position your desk so that you receive fewer interruptions? In the story that opens this workshop, Ozilline tries to stay organized while she watches her coworkers coming and going as she sits at her desk. The furniture arrangement adds to her distraction because her attention is diverted to the action she sees in her peripheral vision.

When furniture is positioned so coworkers can see your face and make eye contact, they are more likely to interrupt you. To avoid this type of interruption, turn your desk so that your back is to others. This will help you stay focused and will discourage people from making idle conversation or interrupting in other ways that prevent you from staying on task.

> " Circumstances may cause interruptions and delays, but never lose sight of your goal. "
>
> —Mario Andretti
> Race Car Driver

♦ *Post a large and visible notice.* As you plan your day, create a time for communicating with your coworkers, and let them know when you're available. Write the information on a board and post it at the entrance to your workspace. The sign should be simple and polite, saying, for example, "I'm busy until 3:30. After that, feel free to stop in with questions. Thank you."

♦ *Be courageous.* You may have to confront some coworkers directly about their frequent interruptions. Let's say you are organizing the company's calendar of events with two other people. It's a complicated job because you must make sure your plan lines up with the work schedules of all the employees. One person you are working with interrupts your concentration often to make personal conversation.

In a case like these, a simple and polite comment usually can stop the interruptions. You might say, "May we talk at lunch. I lose my place when I stop to talk." Or you may need to be more forward, "I don't want you to feel I am not interested in what you are saying, but we have to finish what we're doing without getting sidetracked." If a coworker does not stop interrupting after you have mentioned the matter several times, you may want to ask your supervisor for help with the problem.

Office Noise

Cornell University recently conducted a study on the effect of low-level noise in offices. The University found that low-level noise can actually lower job motivation and increase worker stress. Many office setups make it impossible to avoid low-level noise though, especially the sounds of people talking, computer fans whirring, and other appliances humming.

So how can you keep organized and not let the stress of low-level noise get you down? Several things seem to help. First, instead of listening to the photocopier humming, try listening to classical music on a Walkman™. Another solution is to get out of the office for a few minutes each day. Consider working out at the gym. Exercise is a proven stress buster that can help you relax, stay focused, and build more energy for your organizational tasks.

What Should I Do?

Below is a list of corrections to some typical interruption scenarios. In the blanks, match the correction with the corresponding interruption.

a. Ask to meet with the person after work.

b. Let the coworker know when time is available to talk.

c. Post a note on the door saying, "Please see me at noon, after I'm finished. Thanks."

d. Turn the desk so it faces away from people.

_____ 1. Jill is interrupted four times while she organizes her day.

_____ 2. Andre who can see his colleagues talking finds himself looking at them instead of working on his report due at noon.

_____ 3. Jerry is trying to organize a project due next week, but his friend Taylor keeps coming in to tell him about the trip he and his wife took to Italy.

_____ 4. Oren wants to hear about Laurel's ideas for the project they're both working on, but in order for him to stay organized, he needs to answer his e-mails before lunch, rather than talk to her.

Delays

Delays are common in all workplace situations and, unlike procrastination which you can avoid by changing your own personal habits, or interruptions which can be minimized by dealing directly with the person or people causing them, delays come from hundreds of sources that are often beyond your power to change or are unforeseen and unchangeable.

The more complex the organizational task, the more likely you are to experience time delays. You might have to wait for the supplies to arrive that you need to do a job properly, or you might require the advice of an expert who is busy and hard to reach. If a project lasts a long time, there's more likelihood of delays. Even well meaning, but disorganized, coworkers can cause delays by forgetting deadlines, losing information, or missing important meetings.  Computers can cause delays when they malfunction or when you have to stop to learn an unfamiliar program. So what can you do?

Get back on track. When a deadline is missed, the first item of business is to remain calm. Don't waste time and energy getting upset or pointing fingers.

Part of being organized is looking for creative ways to get things back on schedule when things go wrong. This may mean using a different supplier, adding extra people to get a task completed more quickly, eliminating part of the task, or extending future deadlines.

ACTIVITY 3.3

Dealing with Delays

Several types of delays and possible ways to deal with each delay are described below. Circle the solution you would recommend in each situation.

Molanda must draw a diagram placing furniture in her new office. Her computer program shows several different options, but she can't figure out how the program works. She's wasting time. She should:

    a.   give up.

    b.   ask the computer specialist for help.

    c.   spend more time trying to figure it out herself.

Tamzin is supervising the development of materials for a presentation her company will make at a national conference. At least a dozen of her coworkers are involved in the project. The conference is next week, but a couple of people have had trouble getting important pieces of information, and the whole effort is behind schedule. She should:

    a.   call the conference planner and say that her company will not be presenting.

    b.   ask her employer if she can have the help of a few more of her coworkers to get the job done.

    c.   ask her supervisor for help in getting information from other people.

Carlo is working with Aya to organize charts about their company's annual sales growth. Aya lost a file that contains information they need. Carlo should:

    a.   yell at Aya, and tell her she is incompetent.

    b.   try to complete the chart without all the information needed.

    c.   ask Aya where she last saw the file and help her look for it.

Other Bad Organizing Habits

Besides major problems like procrastination, interruptions, and delays, a few other bad habits can directly influence your ability to organize.

♦ Losing concentration when your work becomes disorganized.

♦ Thinking enough time is available, when it isn't.

♦ Decorating your workspace with distracting items.

Here are ways to recognize that your organizing habits need improvement.

♦ Reliable colleagues tell you so.

♦ You feel totally disorganized.

♦ You can't get anything done.

♦ You often lose things.

Once you identify your bad habits, you can correct them. Try these ways:

♦ Admit that your bad organizing habits are detrimental to your success.

♦ Desire to correct your bad habits.

♦ Think of things you can do to change.

♦ Put your best plan into action.

♦ Start from the beginning if you fall back into bad habits again.

ACTIVITY 3.4

Kicking the Habit

How can you help organize the teacher in the story below. Read the story, then put the responses in the right order by numbering them from 1 to 5.

Wolfram Hartmaan is an African History teacher who loves teaching but hates grading his students' papers. He always puts off grading as long as he can, then carries the papers back and forth from school to home. In the process, he mixes them in with his personal papers.

_____He should want to stop losing papers.

_____He should think about keeping papers in a special box on his desk and leaving them at school or using a special folder for bringing them back and forth.

_____He should recognize that he has a bad habit of losing papers.

_____He should develop a plan for grading.

_____He should schedule a special time for grading.

GETTING CONNECTED

Log on to these web sites for more tips on how to prevent procrastination:

www.endprocrastination.homestead.com

www.ucc.vt.edu/stdysk/procrast.html

Log on to this web site to learn more about avoiding interruptions:

www.wife.org/heard/managetime.htm

Log on to this web site for links to many helpful articles on how to organize and manage time. Click on Organizing (many kinds) or Personal Productivity:

www.mapnp.org/library

WORKSHOP WRAP-UP

- Organization is a process.
- Three obstacles to organization are procrastination, interruptions, and delays.
- The best way to stop procrastinating is to remind yourself that it interferes with good organization.
- Interruptions are common, but easy to manage once you know what to do.
- Delays come from hundreds of sources which are beyond your power.
- If you hit a delay, you should avoid letting it destroy your plan.
- Get back on schedule when things go wrong.

Quick Skills

Diego Fernandez works for the Chamber of Commerce in his town, where he is in charge of creating events that can boost the local economy. When people have ideas for projects, they come to him. His office is filled with papers about both old and new projects. His desk is covered with files about events he hopes to organize one day. Diego doesn't leave his office for lunch—he just orders in—which is why leftovers and soda cans surround his desk.

Everywhere Diego goes, he is given more business cards, flyers, handouts, business forms, and articles. He gets books, mementos, and awards for the events he's conducted, and they're stacking up. While he appreciates these items, he feels like he's living in a haze of clutter. Diego is currently organizing a summer concert series and a film festival. One afternoon, he needs the list of films and presentation materials he prepared for the festival, so he can present the information at a Board Meeting. He remembers receiving the letter in the mail, but he can't find it now. He knows it's somewhere in his office, so he spends a half-hour looking for it.

When he finally finds the letter, many of the materials he was going to use as a part of his presentation are bent and folded. One poster for a new film has a ketchup stain on it. As he enters the meeting late and unprepared, Diego realizes that he needs to make a change in how he organizes his office. He has thought of calling in a professional organizer, but he believes he can get organized himself.

What's Inside

In these pages, you will learn to:

A Neat Workspace

Whether you work in an office, outdoors, or from your home, the efficiency of your workspace plays an important part in how well and how quickly you perform your duties. What is the

condition of your workspace? Is it cluttered with papers, tools, and supplies, or is it neatly arranged in a few stacks? If your work area is messy, or if you often have trouble locating items, here are some steps you can take to organize it.

Step 1: Gather Supplies

Make sure you have the supplies you need for organizing. Your company may provide the necessary supplies, or you may have to purchase them from an office supply store. Get permission from your supervisor or your company's business manager before making the purchase, or you may end up paying for them yourself.

Here are a few of the supplies you will need:

♦ file folders and a pen to mark them
♦ filing cabinets or drawers for storing materials
♦ sturdy and stackable document boxes
♦ a trash can and perhaps a paper recycling bin

Step 2: Set Aside Time

You'll need uninterrupted time to get your work area organized. How much time will depend on how disorganized it is at the start. One to three hours is usually sufficient for most clean-ups.

Step Three: Categorize Items

Classify all the items in your work area and place them in stacks. The following categories can be adapted to any type of work.

1. Work to be accomplished today
2. Work in process
3. Materials to read
4. Papers, supplies, or tools to be stored
5. Items to be discarded

Step Four: Prioritize

With the exception of the discard pile, each stack will contain items to be prioritized. Some tasks, such as mailing a check to a supplier, must be completed as soon as possible. Others may be important, but not require immediate attention. For example, storing supplies is not usually the highest priority.

After you have identified your most urgent projects, ask yourself: Of the things that need to be done today, which must be completed first? Of the documents to read, which should be read first? Some tasks, like filing, should be completed every day. Set aside time at the beginning or end of each day for these chores. Write due dates for

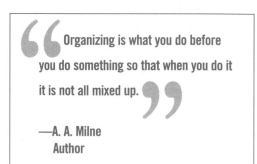

"Organizing is what you do before you do something so that when you do it it is not all mixed up."

—A. A. Milne
Author

projects, appointments, meetings, and other activities on a calendar and review the calendar each day.

Step Five: Discard

If you're a pack rat who hangs on to things you no longer need, now is the time to break the habit. Discard all materials that will never be used again and trash that has accumulated. Here are guidelines for determining which documents can be destroyed.

♦ Throw away paper cups, napkins, and food or drink items near your workspace. Crumbs and spills can ruin documents and seriously damage electronic devices.

♦ Discard items you haven't touched in a long time and don't expect to use in the future, including magazines, junk mail, old reminder notes, and completed "To Do" lists. An interior designer would discard fabric samples, out-of-date catalogs, and rough drafts of designs. In your type of work, what should you discard?

♦ Save documents and supplies that are important, and store them in labeled folders, drawers, or cabinets.

Step Six: Store Everything in Its Place

After you finish organizing, you should have a full trash can and four stacks of items:

1. Work to Be Accomplished Today
2. Work in Process
3. Materials to Read
4. Papers, Supplies, or Tools to Be Stored

Now that you've identified the stacks, your next task is to store the materials properly.

♦ Put finished papers in file folders in your filing cabinets.

♦ Place items to be read on a near-by shelf.

♦ Lay work in process on one side of your desk (or in a drawer or cabinet clearly labeled).

♦ Place work to be accomplished today directly in front of you. Always keep your current project at the front and center of your desk.

You may also want to consider using color-coded file tabs or folders as an aide in organizing. Use one color for new projects and another for existing projects, or try using one color for financial documents and another for correspondence. As the same system will not work in every job, find the system that is best for you.

Step Seven: Stay Organized

Now that you have organized your desk, it's a good idea to set aside time each day to keep the organization up to date. Doing a little every day will eliminate the need for big, time-consuming cleanups.

What's in My Work Area?

Take a look at your work area and identify the categories of items. Fill in the chart below with a list of things you need to organize. If these categories aren't appropriate for your work, substitute your own. When you finish, prioritize the Work to Be Accomplished Today category. List the most important work first, the next most important work second, and so on.

Work to Be Accomplished Today

_____

_____

_____

_____

Priority Order (list the number)

1. _____

2. _____

3. _____

4. _____

Work in Process

_____

_____

_____

_____

Materials to Be Read

_____

_____

_____

_____

Papers, Supplies, or Tools to Be Stored

_____

_____

_____

_____

Items to Discard

_____

_____

_____

_____

A Place for Everything

Everything in your work area should be returned to its proper location after each use. In time, you'll automatically go to this place for the item, just as you automatically hit the car brake pedal with your foot when you need to stop.

Drawers

Drawers are *not* the place to sweep everything from the top of a disorganized desk or table. Use drawers for the small items that can get misplaced easily. A chef might store spatulas, measuring spoons, and ladles in a drawer, and an electrician would need drawers for screws, nails, and small wire. A desk drawer in an office should be used for staples, paper clips, pens and pencils, scissors, and similar items. Follow these guidelines for arranging drawers:

1. Store like items together. Keep the pens with the pens, the pencils with the pencils, and the paper clips with the paper clips.
2. Throw out trash that has accumulated.
3. Return unneeded items to the supply cabinet. Don't keep things that are used infrequently in a desk drawer.
4. Separate items such as staples and paper clips, and place them in small containers before storing them in drawers.

Cabinets

Store large items, such as boxes, electronic equipment, or large cartons in cabinets. Here are a few tips for cabinet storage:

♦ Label the fronts of each box or carton.
♦ Make sure all of the labels are visible. If you stack one box in front of another, you'll hide the second box.

Did you know

Furniture designer Herman Miller discovered that if people enjoy their work environment, they will be more productive. For his designs, he studied how air quality, light, and the arrangement of furniture affect worker performance. He discovered that a well-organized, comfortable, and beautiful workspace provides a sense of well-being for workers. Miller's adjustable chairs fit people of all shapes and sizes, so each person will be comfortable and develop fewer aches and pains. His cabinets and drawers are easily accessible and efficiently organized so that people don't strain their backs reaching for

- Place the most frequently used items in easily reachable places in front, at about chest height.
- Protect materials that aren't used often by placing them in plastic wrap or sealed boxes.
- Place similar items together. For example, keep the cleaning supplies separate from books or electronic equipment.
- Clean the area often if the work you do creates dust or other particles.

Creating and Managing a File System

Creating an efficient filing system that fits the needs of your workplace is a complex task that can be simplified by following a few important guidelines. In this section, you'll learn how to create and maintain an effective filing system.

Organizing Files

Filing cabinets hold a large number of documents on one or several subjects. To keep a filing system organized, you must:

- Label the folder and file drawers clearly.
- Place all documents in their correct folders.
- Return all folders to their original location after they have been used.

Folders in a filing system are grouped together by subject. For example, a sales manager might label three filing drawers this way: one for Clients, another for Sales Reports, and a third for Personnel, while a landscape assistant might label three

drawers as Evergreen Trees, Blooming Trees, and Plants. Two common methods used for filing are alphabetic and numeric, each of which can be subdivided further:

1. *Alphabetic Systems*
   - Correspondence filing (by name)
   - Geographic filing (by city, region or country)
   - Subject filing (by topic or project)
2. *Numeric Systems*
   - Numeric filing (by sequential numbers)
   - Chronological filing (by date)

Alphabetic files

Filing according to the letters of the alphabet is the most common method of organizing folders because it's simple and easy. Alphabetic files can be arranged according to the last names of clients (correspondence); by countries, regions, or city names (geographic); or by the first name of a project (subject). This system works well for jobs where projects are repeated or clients come back year after year.

When enough folders are generated to separate the three types of alphabetic files, each type of folder is filed in a separate drawer, with one for correspondence, another for geographic areas, and another for projects. Review the box on page 49, for examples of both alphabetic and numeric systems.

Numeric files

In a large file system, numeric folders are often helpful. For example, lawyers who see hundreds of clients number their files so that the highest number corresponds to the newest case. They keep an alphabetic list of all clients and their case numbers, then refer to the list for a client's number each time they need a file. For example,

Ramona Sanchez might be assigned the number 11023. Each time her file is needed, the attorney or paralegal locates Ms. Sanchez's name on the alphabetical list and looks in the file drawer for No. 11023. In a chronological system, files are arranged in the drawer by date.

Filing System Samples

Random alphabetic file names	Correct alphabetic order
Mara's Restaurant	Baltimore Orioles
Georgie Campolo	Georgie Campolo
Baltimore Orioles	Jesus's Grocery
Matrix Systems	Mara's Restaurant
Southeast Manor	Matrix Systems
Jesus's Grocery	Southeast Manor
Jeanette Waterman	Jeanette Waterman

Numeric file list		Correct numeric order	
16534	Agosto, Rico	16571	Halbert, Phillipe
16571	Halbert, Phillipe	16547	McNally, Janet
12328	Knight, Peter	16534	Agosto, Rico
16547	McNally, Janet	16521	Zagola, Elma
14983	Olin, Patrice	14983	Olin, Patrice
16521	Zagola, Elma	12328	Knight, Peter

Chronological file list		Correct chronological order	
3/14/02	Cleveland Market	7/17/03	Radnor Center
5/20/02	Medici Skymall	2/6/03	One Trinity Place
2/6/03	One Trinity Place	5/20/02	Medici Skymall
7/17/03	Radnor Center	3/14/02	Cleveland Market
9/7/00	Suarez Plaza	12/01/01	Tarington Bridge
12/01/01	Tarington Bridge	9/7/00	Suarez Plaza

Guidelines for Filing

♦ Label all filing cabinets and drawers. For example, in an alphabetic filing system, the first drawer might be labeled A-L and the second, M-Z. In a numeric system, the first drawer might be labeled 1-150 and the second, 151-300.

♦ Each time you add a file folder to a drawer, write or type a name or number on the folder tab to indicate what information goes in that folder. The labels for every folder should be prepared in the same way so that all files are consistent. See the following section for information on preparing labels.

♦ When you add a new folder or return a folder that has been removed, be sure to place it in its correct alphabetic or numeric spot. Otherwise, the next person who wants to use the file will be unable to find it.

♦ Use color coding for files if you are a visual person. Colored labels separate categories, so the categories are easy to pick out at a glance. For example, a doctor might want to know by glancing at a file whether a patient is an adult or a child. By using a label of one color for adults and of another color for children, this information is immediately visible.

Although color codes are helpful in recognizing a category for the file, they must be used in combination with another system such as alphabetic or numeric. For

Filing System Samples

Alphabetic Filing

    Correspondence

♦ List the last name first, the first name next, and the middle initial or name last on the folder tab. Note: List Mr., Mrs., Professor, Dr., or similar terms as part of the last item on the label (Lopez, Melanie Dr.).

♦ List the name of a business exactly as the name is written.

    Geographic

♦ List the name of the geographic area.

    Subject

♦ List the name of the topic or project.

Numeric Filing

    Numeric with name

♦ List the number only or the number and name of the client or project on the folder tab.

Chronologic Filing

♦ List the date and the project name on the tab. Starting with the year and following with the month and day.

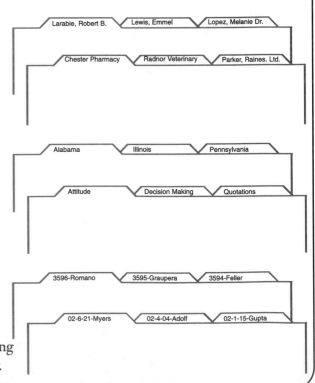

example, adult folders in blue will still need to be alphabetized.

♦ Prioritize important information. If certain clients are especially important because they do a lot of business with your organization, you might consider color coding their files or setting aside a specific drawer for them.

Preparing Labels

Established rules should be used for labels. A quick summary of the rules are given in the chart on page 50. For a fuller understanding of filing rules, refer to an office reference manual.

ACTIVITY 4.2

The File Frenzy

Several companies or organizations are described below. Identify the type of filing system you would recommend for each.

a. alphabetic by last name

b. alphabetic by subject

c. alphabetic by geographic area

d. numeric with name

e. numeric by date (chronologic)

_____1. DeMaso Rafael owns a one-person computer repair firm with 46 customers made up of both individuals and small businesses.

_____2. Transatlantic Sales is a 15,000-person company that divides its sales territories into 428 regions around the world.

_____3. Drs. Eileen and Josef McAlby are married dentists with 1,419 patients between them.

_____4. Mesa Consulting is a small company that divides its customers into three different types: retail, wholesale, and non-profit.

Active and Inactive Files

An active file contains current projects, and an inactive file contains completed projects. Any folder that has not been used in five years should be moved to the inactive file. To decide if a file is active or inactive, ask yourself the following questions:

♦ Do I use this material frequently?
♦ Is this project finished?
♦ Will I need to reference this information during my upcoming project?
♦ Will anyone else in the office need this information soon?

Keep Or Discard?

Many people keep documents for years after they should be discarded. Buying more filing cabinets isn't the answer. A better solution is to discard unimportant or unnecessary papers. The chart below describes common documents people are afraid to throw out and shows how long the documents actually need to be kept.

How often do you sort through your files? Each time a file folder is used, you should discard any materials in it that won't be needed again. Maintaining files this way makes the larger, periodic organization go much more quickly.

Periodic file organization should occur every three to six months, depending on the size of your filing system.

Disposing of Files

The proper way to dispose of large quantities of unnecessary files is to separate the paper from cardboard, take out any staples or paper clips, and recycle them. It is important to keep throwing out files that are no longer needed so that folders do not become clogged and disorganized.

How Long Is Long Enough?

Type of Record	Amount of Time Records Should Be Kept
Personal Tax Records	Keep for 3 to 6 years The IRS can automatically audit a taxpayer's returns for three years from the date the return was filed, and for up to six years if they suspect the taxpayer has underreported gross income by more than 25%. Corporate records are different. If you are in charge of the corporate tax records, ask your firm's tax attorney for advice.
Employee Records	Keep for 4 years This includes personnel files, time-keeping records, payroll, and related materials.
Legal Documents	Keep materials related to civil matters for 6-8 years and materials related to criminal matters for 10 years or more.
Medical Documents	Keep indefinitely

File It!

Arlena works in a travel agency. She just started her job, and the person who worked at the agency before her left files for new clients and previous clients in the same cabinet. Mixed in are brochures for resorts and destination cities and information about several airlines. The folders seem to be alphabetized, but only by the first names of clients and by the names of random hotels. What should Arlena do? Below, write the steps you think she should take to organize the files.

Step 1

_____

_____

Step 2

_____

_____

Step 3

_____

_____

Organizing Shelves

Shelves are used for storing books, displaying products, storing computer disks, or displaying personal items like pictures. If your shelves are disorganized, try these methods for organizing them:

♦ Take off all items and arrange them in categories, such as books, disks, pictures, and statues. Arrange books by subject or author. For example, put all of your office management books on one shelf and all of your computer reference books on another.

♦ Write the book categories on small labels and place the labels at the locations on the shelf where you

intend to store the books in each category. Be sure to leave adequate room. If you own many books on business and only a few books on office policy, you should allow a sensible amount of space for each.

♦ After your books are separated into categories, alphabetize them. This may seem trivial, but it will save time later when you are hunting for a certain article or text.

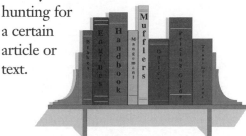

GETTING CONNECTED

For tips on organizing your desk, go to the following web site:

http://www.organizetips.com/office.htm

To learn more about organizing paper files, explore the web site below:

http://www.123sortit.com/BO/paperfiles.html

WORKSHOP WRAP-UP

- Organize a little at the end of each day and week.
- Put files away in their proper place.
- Leave only the current project on your desk.
- Use categories to separate materials that do not belong together.
- Keep active files close by.
- Reorganize your files every three to six months.
- Discard material that is no longer needed.

Celine Devaneau works as an astronomer at a research center in New Mexico. Since she is collecting data about stars, she often works at night using the station's telescope. Her duties include submitting an article to an astronomy journal each month, writing grant proposals to get funding for her project, working on a book she is writing, and making time to be with her family.

She mentions to her coworker Mike Zheng, who works mostly during the day, that it's hard for her to find time for everything because of the strange hours she works. Mike says he has the same problem even though he works a regular 9 to 5 schedule.

They wonder how making time for everything can be so hard. So they decide to brainstorm ways to manage their time. Mike suggests that by comparing schedules they may see ways to increase each other's efficiency.

When they get together, they each make good suggestions. Mike realizes that Celine spends too much time on her book, when she should really be devoting more time to writing grant proposals. They designate a specific time once a week for Celine to work on the book so that she can get to her other tasks on a regular basis. Celine sees that Mike wasted a whole morning waiting for a project from his coworker. When it was late, he didn't use his time efficiently, and he got frustrated with his coworker for setting back his schedule. Celine suggests to Mike that he work on other projects while he waits for materials from others. This way, Mike will get ahead on upcoming projects.

What's Inside

In these pages, you will learn to:

Strategies for Managing Time

You can use a number of strategies to organize your time effectively. Each one will help you improve your job performance, find time to do everything you need to do, and avoid feeling pressured or overwhelmed in the future. Four strategies are described below.

♦ Analyze how you use your time now.
♦ Prioritize the tasks you must accomplish.
♦ Create a schedule.
♦ Do the hardest work when you're at your best.

Analyze How You Spend Time

Before you can improve your time management skills, you need to analyze how you spend your time now. Begin by making a log of everything you do for the next several days. Each time you begin a new activity, write it down. You will have all sorts of things on your list, such as meeting with coworkers, producing work, writing To Do lists, making copies, and opening mail. With each entry, write whether you feel energized, alert, tired, or stressed. Record breaks and meal times, and note what you ate. Record the times of day when you walk or exercise. After a few

days you'll have enough data. Then you can analyze your log and change bad habits that steal your time.

1. Add the amount of time you spend doing each activity.
2. Look for patterns, such as the times of day when you feel alert and the times when you feel tired.

You may be surprised to learn that you spend several hours a week doing unimportant tasks or wasting time. Similarly, you may find that you spend the part of the day when you're the most energized doing non-thinking chores such as opening your mail and downloading e-mail attachments. This means you have to leave the important tasks for when you are tired.

Learn what your habits are and how you can change them to become more efficient. Eat a snack between meals or schedule difficult tasks for after lunch, if your log shows that you work best after consuming food.

Prioritizing

Deciding which items on your To Do list are the most important and doing those things first is called prioritizing. Here are guidelines to help you prioritize effectively:

♦ Calculate how much time you have today.
♦ Make a list of all the things you need to do.
♦ Next to each task, write approximately how much time you think it will take.

The 20/80 Rule

According to the Pareto Principle, 80% of your results will come from focusing on the most vital 20% of a projects's task.

- Place a check mark next to the tasks that must absolutely get done today because of a deadline or other reason. The checked items make up your "hot list."
- Number the tasks on your hot list in order of importance.
- Do task No. 1 first, then task No. 2, and continue until all are finished.
- Complete the items that were not on the hot list.

Occasionally, tasks will be equally important, and you must choose between them. Sometimes, important items from your list won't get done in one day. These should go at the top of the hot list for the next day. If you prioritized correctly, usually you will be able to finish the hot list each day.

Work Hardest at Your Best Times

Some people like to come in early and do the hardest work first. Others, whose energy kicks in later in the day or at night, put off the hardest work until later. From your activity log, you identified the periods when your energy level is the highest and you are the most productive. If your employer allows you to come to work early or stay late, take advantage of this flexibility by aligning your schedule to your preferred work times.

You might want to try taking your work home occasionally. If you do this, be sure everyone who lives with you knows that you are working, so they don't distract you. Putting in long hours at home every day is not a good idea, as you need time to relax and prepare for the next day.

Many businesses expect their employees to start working bright and early. What then? If you have a hard time getting started in the morning, choose items that take less concentration and do them first. Get started on the more challenging items a little later in the day. For example, you may like to answer your e-mail messages or do some reading when you first get to work and begin working on your more complex projects later.

> There's a time for some things, and a time for all things; a time for great things and a time for small things.
>
> —Miguel de Cervantes
> Author

Scheduling Effectively

Once you have figured out what needs to be done in a given period of time, create a schedule that allows time for each task. Remember to save time for routine items, such as answering phone calls or organizing your desk at the end of the day. Assign each item the number of minutes you think will be needed to do the job, and stick to your schedule.

Be sure to schedule breaks, and allow a little extra time for interruptions or delays. Some people fail to schedule meetings and lunch. If you do this, you will soon find yourself feeling rushed, hungry, and behind.

One way to prepare a schedule is to purchase or create a planner that divides the day into 15-minute intervals. To fill in your planner, write the name of the activity beside the time when you will begin working on it. Then draw an arrow to the time when you will finish.

In addition to daily schedules, many people also maintain weekly and monthly schedules. You have probably kept a calendar which showed at a glance what was ahead the rest of the week or month. These calendars are an important resource and should always be kept current.

Make a Schedule

Clarissa must do several things today. Help her schedule them so she allows enough time for each task.

On Fridays, Clarissa arrives at 7 a.m. so she can leave at 3 p.m. and miss the weekend traffic. When she gets into work, she always answers her voice mails and organizes her papers for the first hour. She has a regular staff meeting from 8:30-10:00 a.m. and eats lunch between noon and 12:30 p.m. Today, she has agreed to meet with her coworker, Monique, right after the staff meeting for a half hour. Before lunch, Clarissa likes to spend a half hour working on her e-mails. She should also work on the Poland project for about 45 minutes and the Stakely project for about one and a half hours. Before she leaves, she spends a half hour collecting and turning into the accounting office everyone's time cards for the week.

7:00	
7:30	
8:00	
8:30	
9:00	
9:30	
10:00	
10:30	
11:00	
11:30	
12:00 noon	
12:30	
1:00	
1:30	
2:00	
2:30	
3:00	

Coping with Setbacks and Time Problems

No matter how good you are at prioritizing and scheduling, you can always expect setbacks and delays. Computers malfunction, documents get misplaced, and people become sick. Let's say, for

example, that you are working in the printing business and were given the wrong delivery date for theatre programs. You were told the play is next week, but the

opening performance is actually tomorrow. Suddenly, the programs are your first priority today, but two other projects are also due. How do you handle the situation? Here are ways to react to the unexpected.

Plan Ahead

Always try to stay ahead of schedule. When it comes to working with others, the potential for setbacks increases. Since you can't dictate everyone's schedule, you'll have to use other methods to reduce delays.

- Allow extra time for all major projects.
- Remind coworkers of deadlines.
- If you see someone falling behind, offer to help them catch up.

- Ask for help or put in extra time if you find yourself falling behind.
- Don't panic. If things go wrong, stay calm, put in extra time and get back on track without a fuss.

Out of Time?

Let's say a deadline arrives and you are not finished with your work. Perhaps the project has been delayed through no fault of yours. What will you do? While you'll do your best to avoid such situations, sometimes they will be beyond your control.

To avoid upsetting your supervisor, you'll need to have a plan.

- Apologize, but only once. Don't belittle yourself. That bothers other people and makes the problem seem worse than it is.
- Explain what happened clearly and calmly.
- Suggest ideas for completing the work quickly.
- Ask if the deadline can be extended.
- Ask what action your supervisor would like you to take.
- Do not bring up the incident again, once it is resolved.

Lost time is never found again.

—Benjamin Franklin

These steps work equally well for every profession. While it's natural to be upset or embarrassed when you miss a deadline, letting the problem get you out of balance can create bigger problems. Fix the situation and move on.

Never try to pretend you didn't know when you missed a deadline or say that you have finished a job when you haven't. This is lying, and it will get you into far more trouble than admitting your mistake and fixing it quickly and honestly.

Use Waiting Time Effectively

If you travel frequently or meet with people who have heavy schedules, you may spend a lot of time waiting. Always carry work that you can do in short spurts of time between appointments or when you are confined to a train or plane seat.

- ✓ Read technical journals.
- ✓ Make business calls from your cell phone.
- ✓ Bring a notebook and plan a project.
- ✓ Do computer work.
- ✓ Write letters.
- ✓ Update your electronic calendar.
- ✓ Proofread documents that you must approve.
- ✓ Study reference materials.

ACTIVITY 5.2

Setback

Read the case study about Abdul and circle the right answer for each statement. Then prioritize the order in which Abdul should accomplish each circled item.

Abdul is a hotel employee learning how to manage his time effectively. Today, he was supposed to have the monthly budget and occupancy assessment completed, but he ran out of time. He needs a day to type the data so it is presentable, but he is a very slow typist. He knows he wouldn't have gotten so far behind if only he could type faster.

1. The first thing Abdul should do is:
   a. tell his boss he is a terrible employee.
   b. take a typing class.
   c. leave town.
   d. calmly apologize to his supervisor.

2. The second thing Abdul should do is:
   a. explain to his boss that this happened because he has trouble typing.
   b. repeatedly tell his boss how sorry he is.
   c. blame another employee.
   d. pretend nothing happened.

3. The third thing Abdul should do is:
   a. suggest that his boss fire him.
   b. say that he is afraid this will happen on other projects.
   c. state that the job could be completed more quickly if someone else typed.
   d. suggest that he be given a raise.

4. The fourth thing Abdul should do is:
   a. ask for a different assignment.
   b. say he can't do any more typing.
   c. ask what his supervisor would like him to do.
   d. apologize again.

5. The fifth thing Abdul should do is:
   a. sign up for a typing course.
   b. remedy the situation the best way he can.
   c. take the rest of the day off.
   d. do what his boss has asked as quickly and efficiently as possible.

6. The sixth thing Abdul should do is:
   a. remind everyone how he once got the monthly report out even later.
   b. bring up how bad a typist he is.
   c. get back to work and never miss a deadline again.
   d. make fun of another employee to take the focus off his own mistake.

Time Management Tools

Most people use a combination of time management tools to keep themselves organized. Find items that work well for you by asking friends and coworkers what they use and experimenting with the tools they suggest. Electronic time management devices are becoming increasingly popular, but they are not for everyone. The old-fashioned paper and pen method of scheduling can work well also.

The main thing is to correctly use the tools you choose. If you try a computer calendar but keep missing appointments because you don't understand how to use it, get someone to teach you how to use it properly. You could also buy a paper calendar. It's not important whether your tools are high tech or traditional.

Time Management Tricks

Everyone has learned a trick or two when it comes to managing time. Ask around, and you will find out just how your coworkers keep themselves on schedule. Here are some ideas you should try:

- ◆ Fool yourself into thinking time is passing faster than it is.
- ◆ Double up on similar tasks.
- ◆ Establish routines.
- ◆ Don't do the same work twice.
- ◆ Delegate as many responsibilities as possible.

Psychological Tricks

Have you ever tried turning your watch ahead a few minutes so you will think it's later than it is? Doing this will help you get to appointments on time. Although you will never really forget that your watch or clock is set ahead, looking at the time fools the part of your mind that responds to time pressure. This also works well for meeting project and assignment due dates. Try writing on your calendar a due date that's a few days earlier than the actual date. If you have a tendency to run late on projects, this may help you learn to be early.

Double Up

Have you ever walked to the supply closet for a pen, then returned to your desk and realized you needed a few other supplies. Going back and forth is a waste of time. When you have a group of errands or

Time Management Tool

Try using an erasable whiteboard calendar. This is like a regular calendar but without the pictures. The erasable feature makes it useful because you don't have to get a new one each month or year.

similar tasks, do them all at once. If two different tasks require the same resources, do them one after the other. This is called doubling up. If the printer and FAX machine are next to each other and you need to print a document and send a FAX, do these tasks at the same time. Don't make unnecessary trips back and forth.

Establish Routines

Everyone has times of day where they struggle to stay focused at work. The best way to deal with this time is to form useful habits that allow you to get simple daily chores out of the way.

Experts say it takes eleven days of doing the same activity to form a habit, so give yourself plenty of time to get used to your routine. Soon your body and mind will start these chores automatically. You might use this time to listen to phone messages, respond to memos, and tidy up your desk. Be sure to do these tasks in the same order in the same way at about the same time each day. Soon they will become second nature to you.

Don't Do the Same Work Twice

Use labels, form letters, and other pre-printed materials to keep from having to retype common documents. You should never find yourself in a situation where you are typing or writing the same things over and over again. Once is enough.

Delegate Responsibility

After you break projects into smaller parts, you will see which of the parts could be done by other people. Often, tasks such as researching, memo writing, and document copying can be done by others. Getting them to take over the small chores will free you to tackle the bigger issues.

> Until you value yourself, you won't value your time. Until you value your time, you will not do anything with it.
>
> —M. Scott Peck
> Psychologist and Author

Time and Again

Read each of the job descriptions below, then answer the question, or give the worker advice on how to move forward.

1. Rhonda has two jobs. She teaches English as a Second Language, and she works in the financial aid office of the university where she attends night classes. Many errands crop up in both jobs. She often finds herself wasting time by forgetting to do one or two errands and having to go back out again. What advice would you give her?

   _____

   _____

2. Gunther works at AppleBell, a market research firm, where his morning tasks usually include answering e-mails, returning a few calls, and responding to memos. Gunther tries not to procrastinate, but the mornings are always a sluggish time of day for him. What can Gunther do to keep moving along with his morning priorities?

   _____

   _____

3. Keshawn is an administrative assistant at a financial planning firm. He prepares many of the mailings his firm sends out to its clients. The client list includes two hundred names, which Keshawn types on each envelope every time a mass mailing goes out. How can he reduce the time he spends addressing letters?

   _____

   _____

4. Miranda is a bioengineer. She works on a project which will show how fruit plants can be protected from parasites by using organic methods. She has broken the project into parts: research to be done, quotes to be gathered, and a report to write. What can Miranda do to free her time so she can work on the research instead of spending a lot of time on the other project components?

   _____

   _____

5. Albert always seems to be running behind for meetings and appointments. He knows that when he arrives late he looks disorganized. What can he do to get himself places on time?

   _____

   _____

GETTING CONNECTED

If you want to think more about time itself, and time management in particular, you can search for the term "time management" using an Internet search engine. You may also want to check out the following site:

http://www.mindtools.com/page5.html

WORKSHOP WRAP-UP

- Prioritizing is the best way to organize your time.
- Scheduling your priorities will help you meet deadlines.
- Never try to cover up if you run out of time on a project.
- Choose supplies that will help you manage your time well.
- Use time tricks to stay on track.
- Everyone has times of day when focusing is difficult.
- Delegate small tasks to others when possible.

WORKSHOP 6

Genji has been working for a technology design firm for almost four years. Hired right out of college, she has worked hard to develop her organizational skills by going to workshops, learning from coworkers, and putting all the new ideas to work. Her desk is always neat, and she makes a point of getting back to clients and supervisors quickly. She keeps track of deadlines and schedules effectively.

Her hard work is paying off because just this week she was asked to head the design team for a special project. Her company is entering a contest to build a solar powered car and race it across the country. Most of the company's major competitors are also entering in the race, so this is a good opportunity for Genji's company to exhibit its technological skill and creative know-how.

The winning car's company will receive a large cash award and a lot of media attention. Genji is honored to have been selected to head the team, and she realizes her company is depending on her. She is a little concerned about working on such a large and public project. Until now, she's mainly been a behind-the-scenes person.

She wants to prepare herself to organize the details, so she enrolls in a seminar on project management. She also attends a meeting offered by the group sponsoring the competition. Just to be sure she hasn't missed anything, Genji checks out materials about organizing major projects from her local library. When she arrives at her office on Monday, her boss asks whether she feels overwhelmed with her assignment. Genji smiles and answers, "No, I think I have it under control." She's learned to use everything she has at her disposal to become an outstanding organizer.

What's Inside

In these pages, you will learn to:

Before You Begin a Project

Many people, when they are first assigned to a project, want to get to work right way

gathering information and materials. All this effort can be wasted if a plan for how to proceed is not in place. Like laying the foundation of a house, a well-organized project is built on thoughtful and detailed planning. Here are four steps that will help you plan.

1. Set goals.
2. Establish a plan.
3. Break the project into manageable parts.
4. Create a realistic schedule.

Skipping these steps will result in a poor final project or one that doesn't get completed.

Decide on Your Goals

Occasionally, project goals will be given to you by your supervisor, but other times you will be expected to develop them on your own. You'll need to ask a few questions before you can decide what the goals for a project should be.

1. What is the purpose of this project?
2. What product or services will the project provide?
3. Who will benefit from this project?
4. How much time and money is available to do the work?
5. Who are the main people responsible for seeing this project through to its conclusion?
6. What form will the completed project take?

Once you can answer all these questions, you are ready to move on to the next preliminary planning step.

Establish a Plan

The second step in organizing a project is figuring out exactly what will be required to get the job done right, on budget, and on time.

1. Who will provide the supplies?
2. Will more than one supplier be necessary?
3. What are the supplier's cost estimates?
4. Has enough money been allocated to the project?
5. Approximately how many hours will the project take?
6. Can the company afford the necessary hours?
7. Are any materials, supplies, data, or information unavailable?
8. Can the project be done without the unavailable items?

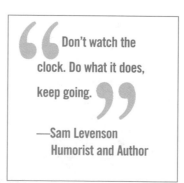

66 Don't watch the clock. Do what it does, keep going. 99

—Sam Levenson
Humorist and Author

If the materials or funds are not available, it is time to go back to the first step and develop new project goals.

Break the Project into Parts

Once you establish your goals and identify the materials needed, the next step is to break the project down into parts. If it's a team project, you will need to assign each part to the best person for the job. For example, if a suspension bridge needs to be built and one team member is a design engineer, it makes sense to assign the design work to this person.

After you decide who should do what, you need to establish priorities. For a bridge, the first priorities will be to develop designs and obtain building permits. Later, you will be ready to begin construction.

By the time you assign all parts of a project, every team member should be clear about who is doing what, the materials that will be needed, the completion date, and the procedures that are to be followed. Be sure you know the answers to: Who? What? When? How?

Create a Schedule

When your responsibilities for a project are clear, create a schedule to meet your time deadlines. If you are the project manager, ask each team member to do the same and require strict adherence to the deadlines.

You will need to merge the new project with your other daily responsibilities, such as attending meetings and keeping your regular appointments.

You should let people know when you are working on a new project. This gives you and them a chance to reschedule appointments around the extra work.

If possible, you should complete your other projects before beginning a new one. Allow more time than you think you will need. In this way, you will have breathing room if something gets delayed. Once you make a schedule, stick to it. If changes are needed, you can reevaluate.

? Did you know

When people work on large projects, they often try to get more done than is scheduled on a given day. They think that they will have less to do the next day. It is better to go home early and get some rest than to stay late and run the risk of exhausting yourself.

ACTIVITY 6.1

Planning a Project

As an assistant in the administrative office of a large hospital, you have been asked by your supervisor to confirm the purchase date and serial number of all 240 patient beds. Your supervisor needs the project completed and a brief report prepared within three weeks. Complete the chart below to show your understanding of the project.

Goal: _____

Materials needed: _____

_____

_____

The parts of the project: _____

_____

_____

_____

The schedule: _____

_____

_____

_____

Getting Started

Once planning for a project is complete, you are ready to implement it. Some people feel overwhelmed when starting a new project and have trouble getting going. To avoid this, work on small, manageable pieces and allow yourself an appropriate amount of time to do each.

Keep your focus on the small tasks. While understanding the big picture is important, you may feel stressed if you concentrate on the big picture too much. Motivate yourself by identifying a personal reward for completing each piece of the job. Appropriate awards might include an occasional afternoon's vacation or lunch with the team.

Keeping up and using your creativity are keys to continuing success after you get started.

THE START

Keeping Up

Since you learned in Workshop 5 how to use a planner or calendar to establish a schedule, you should be able to meet most deadlines. If you encounter a problem, be creative in finding a way to get back on track quickly. Ask for help if you need it.

Managers and supervisors prefer to know when an employee needs help, rather than finding out later after a deadline is missed. By asking for help, you will get the assistance you need, learn how to handle a similar situation the next time, and distinguish yourself by showing the good judgment to identify your need.

Show Your Creativity

Employers appreciate workers who come up with innovative solutions to problems. If you know a way to get a certain part of the project completed more efficiently or quickly than has been proposed, speak up. Good organizational ideas go to waste if you assume no one wants to hear them.

Reasons Projects Fail

The trouble with many projects is that they never get completed. The reasons for this vary. Perhaps a very important piece of information can't be found, or supplies are not available. Often, projects get abandoned because a system for completion is not in place. The following section explains further why projects fail and how you can organize for a successful conclusion.

Too Many Projects

Try not to start several new projects at once. While managing multiple projects is often necessary, you should plan them in advance and combine them into a schedule that affords enough time for each to be completed accurately and fully. Sometimes a new idea will come to you in the middle of a project, and you'll want to act on it. Control this impulse or your original project will suffer. Here's how to avoid this problem:

1. When new ideas appear, note them and save them in a folder marked Future Projects. You may want to put each idea in a separate folder.
2. Stay focused on the current project. Ignore distractions or remove yourself from the situation.
3. Test, on the current project, any relevant new ideas.
4. Be patient. To make something happen you must first imagine it, then allow time to do the work. This takes you from the dream to the reality.

> 66 You will never FIND time for anything. If you want time, you must make it. 99
>
> —Charles Buxton
> Author

Poor Communication

Projects sometimes fall apart because the communication between team members is poor. Keeping a project well organized means staying in touch with everyone involved. People can be reached almost anywhere by telephone, cell phone, e-mail, regular mail, FAX, or voice mail. There is no excuse for not communicating.

Let's say that you work for a graphic design firm, and your client needs a hundred baseball caps embroidered for the company picnic. Here are steps to take to keep everyone in the communication loop:

1. Identify the client's preferred design and colors.
2. Communicate the specifications clearly to the designer.
3. Show the design and a sample hat to the client and get approval to continue.
4. Submit the design and the order to the embroidery factory project manager and establish a deadline for delivery.

If you do not communicate clearly, your client may end up with the wrong colors or the wrong design. To communicate fully and accurately, try using these guidelines:

1. Listen carefully.
2. Write down important facts and dates.
3. Obtain a signed approval from the client.

4. Require sign-offs at each stage of the process.
5. Ask for feedback to be sure everyone understands. This may seem simple, but very often people misinterpret both verbal and written communication.

Lack of Creative Thinking

Sometimes when one thing goes wrong with a project, the whole project collapses. To overcome this problem, you'll need to think in new ways—to look at the whole situation objectively, as if you were an outside observer. Consider the following example: a truck is too tall and gets stuck going under an overpass. Traffic is backed up for miles, and no one knows what to do. The truck can't move forward or backward. Finally, a little girl in one of the cars says to her mother, "Why don't they let some air out of the tires?" Her mother leans out her window and shouts the idea forward. Finally, the truck driver gets the message. He tries the idea and it works.

Children are especially good at creative thinking, but anyone can do it. Ask yourself these questions:

1. How would I evaluate this situation if I weren't involved?
2. Are there any simple solutions I haven't considered?
3. What novel ways for handling this situation might work?

Insufficient Follow-Up

When a project is completed, it usually goes through a process of evaluation by a supervisor to see if it meets the goals. If it doesn't, the supervisor will ask for a correction or additional work. Your responsibility includes staying with the project until it is completed to the supervisor's and the customer's requirements.

Once the project has been approved, thank everyone who contributed. If someone did an especially good job, send a complimentary note to the person and a copy to the individual's supervisor. If a person worked hard but had trouble doing his or her part, provide words of encouragement, acknowledging the effort. Being recognized in front of others is one of the most sincere forms of flattery. Try this techniques with your coworkers and watch the result.

Reorganizing Another's Project

People leave projects for a variety of reasons. They may take medical absence, get called away to another assignment, change departments, or move to another city. Whatever the case, being asked to take over someone else's work can be a real challenge. Deadlines for completing the project may already be set, or you may have a hard time sticking to a schedule that is based on someone else's organizational strengths, weaknesses, and time management skills. Here are some ways to reorganize when you inherit a partially completed project.

1. Take the time to read and learn everything you can about the project.
2. Try to be in touch with the person who began the project. Come prepared with a list of questions such as:

   ♦ Are any of these dates and times flexible?
   ♦ Are other materials available to read about what's needed?
   ♦ Can the work be changed to reflect my own organizational style?

> " A lot of our busy-ness is a way for us to avoid thinking about what is most important. There's a difference between being busy and being productive. "
>
> —Kristen Lippincott
> Direct of the Royal Observatory

ACTIVITY 6.2

Creating Solutions

You have just taken over as project manager for a trucking company in New York. You need to use your creativity and communication skills to solve a problem. Analyze the problem below and write what you would do.

Your carrier service delivers lettuce from California to New York in the winter. Because of snowy weather, delays have occurred, and the lettuce leaves are turning brown. Four of the twenty trucks have broken down. Now, three of the drivers are out with the flu and a blizzard is predicted to hit during the upcoming week. You have received multiple calls from grocery store owners all over the city complaining that their deliveries are late. What should you do to serve your customers better?

Step 1: _____

_____

_____

_____

Step 2: _____

_____

_____

_____

Step 3: _____

_____

_____

_____

Step 4: _____

_____

_____

_____

Step 5: _____

_____

_____

_____

Quick Skills

Managing Multiple Projects

Having too much to do occurs for many reasons. Perhaps you take on too many projects, your company or department is understaffed, or your supervisor assigns you a heavy load. If you feel overwhelmed by too much work, certain organizing skills can help you manage the load more effectively.

◆ Stay on task.
◆ Reduce distractions.
◆ Eliminate personal interferences, such as phone calls.
◆ Delegate or share responsibilities if possible.

When you have too much to do, you hit task overload. The more you try to juggle, the less efficient you become at performing any single task. Similarly, the longer you wait before returning to an interrupted task, the harder it is to remember where you left off. Not surprisingly, all this leads to stress and diminishes productivity. The following discussion will help you when you have too much work.

Don't Rely on Memory

If you try to remember everything, sooner or later you'll get mixed up. Use a simple backup system such as jotting notes on a pad of paper or installing computer tracking software. Transferring what's in your head to an external system allows you to concentrate on more important matters.

Learn to Estimate Time

Mistakes occur when people start to run out of time. By estimating time accurately, you can meet deadlines, eliminate mistakes, and reduce stress. Before you start a task, write the amount of time you think will be needed to complete it. Time yourself from the minute you start until the minute you finish. Check the actual time against your estimate. Was the estimate correct or did you underestimate? In the future, adjust your estimates based on the time differences you discovered.

Reducing Priority Overload

✓ Keep lists of the tasks you must accomplish.
✓ Assign each task an order of importance.
✓ Give yourself a specific amount of time for each task.
✓ When you finish one task, cross it off your list and put it out of your mind.

Finish What You Start

The most fulfilling way to work is to persevere until a task is done. This may require removing distractions. Turn off the ringer on the phone or let the answering machine get it. Post a note on your door to let coworkers know when you will be able to talk to them again. Find a private room where you can work without interruptions.

Switch Tasks Effectively

Task switching is the ability to drop what you are doing and move on to something else that has become more important. Projects need to be reordered for a variety of reasons. For example, a client calls and needs a job finished more quickly than had been anticipated. A coworker goes home sick and someone else has to take over his or her work. When you have to switch tasks, try these ways to keep your balance:

♦ Take a few minutes to make notes about what you had been working on, recording important points about the job.

♦ Take a quick break, so that you can clear your head and start fresh on the new task.
♦ Think about the new task and forget about what you were working on before.
♦ Figure out how long the new task will take, so that you can adjust your schedule and still accomplish all the other tasks for which you are responsible.

Establish a Routine

Managing multiple tasks is easier when you establish a routine that allows you to work automatically. When you repeat a task daily, the creative part of your brain is not needed. It is free to deal with more complex tasks. For example, most people drive automatically. They listen to music or engage in conversation while they step on the gas and turn the wheel of their car. You can create similar routines at work.

Did you know

When the American astronaut Jerry Linenger was working aboard the MIR space station, he wore three or four watches with alarms set to let him know when to switch tasks.

Quick Skills

Organizing Multiple Projects

Chances are that you manage several different projects each day. In Column 1, list each project that needs work today. Then in Column 2, write the tasks that you will accomplish for each project.

Project   Task

_____   _____

                                                 _____

                                                 _____

                                                 _____

_____   _____

                                                 _____

                                                 _____

                                                 _____

_____   _____

                                                 _____

                                                 _____

                                                 _____

_____   _____

                                                 _____

_____   _____

                                                 _____

GETTING CONNECTED

To find more information on organizing projects, try typing "project organization" into your search engine. You can also consult the following web site for more resources. Take a look at these helpful articles for some more ideas on project management.

http://www.ee.ed.ac.uk/~gerard/Management/

WORKSHOP WRAP-UP

- Every project is different.
- Set project goals, find the materials you need, and schedule your time so you can complete all the parts.
- Organization is the foundation of effective projects.
- Ask for help when you need it.
- Think creatively.
- Don't get distracted.
- Make sure you follow through.
- Put your thoughts on paper to free your mind to think.
- Making common tasks routine gives you more time to think about complex tasks.

Quick Skills

Ramona looks at her computer and groans. Stored somewhere in the vast memory of her hard drive are three documents which she is supposed to e-mail to a client today. Where are they? She thought she put all three in the same file, but she can't remember which file.

When she tries to run the Find Document function, she can't remember what she called the documents, so the computer can't bring them up.

She doesn't remember saving them to a disk. Even if she had, she probably wouldn't have labeled the disk. She usually has to go through one disk after another to find what she needs.

Javier, the technical support person, sees Ramona looking upset, and he stops by her office. She explains the problem, and Javier finally finds the documents. He tells her that she needs to label all her documents for a single project in a similar way. He says to use easy-to-remember, practical titles. He reminds her to back up important work on disks and to make sure she keeps her current project files on her desktop where they can be easily accessed.

As he leaves he adds, "When you set up your files, keep them simple. Imagine someone else trying to find a document on your computer. Make the system easy enough that they'd know just where to look."

Ramona feels relieved after she talks to Javier. She's known for some time that her computer needs organizing, but she didn't know how to go about it. She has to admit that she's lazy about making back ups. She's learning the hard way how important it is to properly organize her computer files.

What's Inside

In these pages, you will learn to:

Organizing Your Desktop

Most people know what an organized desk looks like, but what about an organized computer desktop? Even though computers are widely used, the technology changes so rapidly that many people do not know how to keep their files up to date.

Just like the top of your office desk, your computer desktop needs to be neat too. The background of your desktop can look any way you want, from pictures of your family to a plain blue screen. It's what's on top that counts.

Unlike an actual desk, which can be cleaned of absolutely everything, a computer desktop will always have a few items on it, including the hard disk icon, a trash can, a tool bar, and several special programs which cannot be removed. Other items that belong on the desktop include:

♦ folders for current projects
♦ links to the Internet
♦ folders for documents you receive as e-mail attachments
♦ personal folders or a document or two

The key to a neat desktop is keeping only what you need, not cluttering it with lots of "loose" documents or unimportant icons. Things that don't belong on the desktop include:

♦ documents that belong in specific files
♦ icons for games or programs that you aren't using
♦ files for old, closed, or completed projects

Remove or file in another location any folders that are inactive. Don't try to remove everything from your desktop. Some of the files are programs that keep the computer running! If you don't recognize an item, ask someone to identify it before you put it in the trash.

Keep It Simple

Even though you are the primary user of your computer, a supervisor or coworker may need to obtain a document or information while you are out. For this reason, it is essential to use clearly labeled and easily understandable titles for all documents and folders, especially those important ones on your desktop.

Some people, especially creatively minded ones, tend to give their files and documents unusual names. Suddenly, a document which should be labeled "Letter to Rosamond Azul" gets titled "Really Rosie" or "let2RA." Someone else would

> " I do not fear computers. I fear lack of them. "
>
> —Isaac Asinoz
> Science Fiction Author

have a hard time guessing what is contained in these documents by looking at their titles. Not only that, but if a document gets misplaced in a computer and you want to use the Find feature to retrieve it, you must be able to remember the whole name of the document or file.

Unless you have some system for naming documents and files, your computer will become as disorganized as a paper strewn desk. Here are simple steps to follow for naming documents:

♦ Name things what they are. For example: letters, folders, outlines, or invoices.

♦ Be very clear about the name. You can shorten words, but don't abbreviate them so much that you can't identify the file when you search for it.

♦ Give all things that go together a similar title. If you have a series of files that all relate to one project called Rotel, the title of every document having to do with the project should begin with the word Rotel, followed by a short description of that document.

For example, Rotel-project outline, Rotel-letter to Steven Wallace 3/23, and Rotel-document from Janice Mills 4/14 are all useful names.

♦ Include dates of documents in their titles if the descriptions are similar. This is especially important for letters sent and received.

♦ Consider using an easily understood abbreviation when you don't want to write out the entire project name, for example, "AG Park Proj" for the project name "Anderson-Goodbody Memorial Park Project."

♦ Date or number earlier drafts of documents to indicate which draft they represent.

Ergonomics

When you work on a new computer, be sure the keyboard is at a comfortable height so you don't have to crane or twist your neck to see the monitor. Adjust your chair so that you can relax with your feet flat on the floor. This reduces the risk of stress injuries and increases the blood flow to allow you to be more productive while working on your computer.

ACTIVITY 7.1

Useful Names

Several computer documents and suggested names are given below. Which name is better to keep these documents organized? Circle your first choice.

Project's Actual Name	Possible Name	Possible Name
1. Grace Robin Benefit	GR Benefit	Gracie Ben
2. Oklahoma Waste Management Project	Okie WM	OK Waste Proj
3. Nelson Field Research	Nelie's Notes	Nelson Proj
4. University Catalogue	University Cat	U. Catalogue
5. New York Market Sales Report	NYMarSalRe	NY Sales

List four actual projects you're handling at work or school. Write an appropriate computer title.

Project's Actual Name	Descriptive Shorter Title
1. _____	_____
2. _____	_____
3. _____	_____
4. _____	_____
5. _____	_____

Folders and Documents

All computer documents should be saved in folders. If a folder contains so many documents that it is hard to find what you need, establish folders within the folder to hold documents that go together. For example, a folder labeled Client Orders might contain orders from 100 different clients. When a file is this long, it's hard to find a specific order. You should set up separate alphabetic subfolders such as A-D, E-L, M-R, and S-Z. Hundreds of documents can be broken down and organized into just a few manageable folders.

- Name folders and documents with an easy-to-remember title.
- Break long lists of documents into subfolders within the primary folder.
- Put all new documents into the proper folder as soon as you create or receive them.

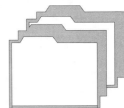

Ready to become a computer folder expert? Here are a few extra tips to help you organize your folders like a pro:

♦ You can often choose the color of your computer folders. Always use the same color for the same type of files—current files, personal files, inactive files, and so on—or try using different colors for different projects.

♦ Most computers allow you to view the items contained in a folder in several different ways: as a list, as icons, as a list sorted by date, or as list sorted by name. View lists in the way that's easiest for you.

♦ Remove old or completed projects from your desktop. Put them away in a folder for completed work.

♦ Empty your recycling bin/trash of all folders and documents you don't need. Some trash bins don't automatically empty, so they use disk space you need for other files.

Saving

Any number of events can cause you to lose power to your computer, including a storm, a blown fuse, someone accidentally unplugging the computer, or a power surge. When the power goes out, you may loose a substantial amount of the information you have stored on your hard-drive, including client information, letters, documents, and records. At the very least, you will definitely loose any unsaved material you were working on at the time of the power loss. A few small organizational habits can save you worry and wasted time if this happens. First, save everything you are working on every fifteen minutes or so. That way, when the power goes out, you only have to redo fifteen minutes of work, not hours and hours. Many programs have an auto-save function. Be sure this function is turned on if you have it.

? Did you know

Never consume food or drinks near your computer. Spilled beverages can cause serious computer malfunctions, and sandwich crumbs can make your keyboard sticky. This causes problems that waste time or cost money to fix.

Periodically save all your important computer files to floppy disks. You need to remember a few tips:

- Floppy disks get old and develop disk errors, so use new ones each time you back up your files.
- Save everything to disk about once a week. Set a date and time to do this chore so you don't forget.
- Store disks in a cool, safe place. Use the same location each time so you won't forget it. If files on disks contain confidential information, follow your office policy about storing them.

E-mail

Organizing your e-mail is easy if you use the tools your computer provides, such as e-mail filters, e-mail filing cabinets, and download or attachment folders.

E-mail filters

Most e-mail programs enable you to set up filters for your incoming messages. This means you type in the names and e-mail addresses of the people who are likely to send e-mail and group them into categories, such as coworkers, clients, and family. Your computer automatically filters all your messages into these categories when a message with a recognizable name appears.

You can update your filters as needed. The time spent setting up your filters is insignificant compared to the amount of time you save. You don't have to figure out which of the messages in a large jumble of unorganized mail are the important ones. Filters enable you to:

1. See at a glance who has sent you what.
2. Quickly recognize important e-mails that require an immediate response.
3. Keep you from overlooking something important.

E-mail filing cabinets

Wouldn't it be great to have a record of every e-mail you sent and received so you could bring up information any time you needed it? You can do this by setting up or enabling your e-mail filing cabinet. Instead of having to cut and paste every message into a new word document in order to save it, your computer automatically saves to a file cabinet every message you haven't deleted. Just remember—computer filing cabinets can fill up quickly, so you need to set aside a few minutes each month to delete unneeded items. That way, the filing cabinet won't become chaotic or so big it slows down your computer! Read your software manual to learn how to use e-mail filing cabinets.

Practice Using Filters

Think of names for 3 or 4 categories you would use to group the following e-mail messages for Becky Margolis, who works at Arkoplane Publishing House. Becky receives messages from clients, vendors, friends, family, and other acquaintances. She wants to establish filters for her e-mails. Write at the bottom of the page the category names you recommend for each message, then place the number of each e-mail in its correct category.

E-mail address	Message
1. hkck@spark.com	Happy Birthday Sweetheart- Love Mom
2. bcj9@arkoplane.org	Please answer my question by noon
3. adbo@ppi.com	New Products For Publisher
4. matt@link.com	Becky- Happy B-day Sis!
5. miltongoen@oster.com	Becky, did you send the new chapter?
6. qrt@arkoplane.org	New Workplace Harassment Guidelines
7. gabrielozzart@tannerger.com	The information you requested regarding copyrights
8. Superpaper@aol.com	Paper to Purchase for Publishing Houses
9. maria@margolis-zinker@town.com	To My Favorite Niece- Congrats!
10. rs14@arkoplane.org	Come see me during your lunch break
11. adelocoort@pagota.com	B- I'm sending the first 50 pages tomorrow
12. roglow@martinet.com	Supplies for writers, editors, publishers!
13. joel@lightnet.com	Happy 39 from your Gramps
14. prunellamoses@gladheart.com	Final read through looks good. I'll call Monday.
15. ztech@bgi.com	Books on latest publishing advances
16. ms49@arkoplane.org	Employee lunch tomorrow

Name of Category _____ Message Number:_____

Name of Category _____ Message Number:_____

Name of Category _____ Message Number:_____

Name of Category _____ Message Number:_____

Keeping Pace and Troubleshooting

Computer problems can waste your time and throw you off schedule, which puts your project behind and makes you scramble to keep up. To stay on schedule, you must know how to keep yourself and your computer working quickly and efficiently.

When your computer runs slowly or crashes, it is often a sign that it is disorganized.

Speed

Several things will make your computer run faster including:

♦ more memory
♦ low disk fragmentation
♦ small number of windows open

Memory

To increase your computer's memory without buying expensive new chips, you can eliminate excess files by deleting them or saving them to a disk. If you are uncertain whether a document should be deleted, check with your technical support person or supervisor. Auto-filing systems and unused programs often take up a lot of memory, so try to clear these out first.

Fragmenting

When documents are saved, computers often misplace bits of information, storing them in the wrong places. This is called fragmenting. It is perfectly normal and usually not noticeable, but it may cause your computer to slow down or crash more often. Fortunately, many operating systems come with a disk defragmenter that you can run to correct the problem. This takes a while so you might want to start the program as you head off to lunch or to a meeting. Defragmentation should be finished by the time you return. You will only need to run this program every few months, but you should schedule it on your calendar so your computer always runs smoothly and efficiently.

Windows

The more windows or programs you have open, the more items the computer will have to manage at once. Of course, it is the computer's job to handle many programs, but it may slow down or crash if you run too many programs at the same time. Just as you only keep the items you are currently using on your office desk, train yourself to keep open only the computer programs you are using.

? Did you know

Magnets and computers don't mix. Magnets can ruin computer monitors and floppy disks! Many an employee has put magnetic items near their computer with disastrous results.

Help the Computer User

Joanne Zimmerman, an administrative assistant at a newspaper, needs help deciding how to correct the following problems with her computer. What advice will you give her?

1. She keeps getting a "Not enough memory for this function" message when she tries to open her e-mail. The following programs are open: Microsoft® Word, Excel, Access, and Publisher.

   _____

   _____

   _____

   _____

2. The computer has crashed three times today. She has a busy day and doesn't believe she has time to run the defragmentation program.

   _____

   _____

   _____

   _____

3. Joanne's files have accumulated over the three years she's used her computer. She's afraid to delete any files because she's not sure which are important.

   _____

   _____

   _____

   _____

> You go to your TV to turn your brain off. You go to the computer when you want to turn your brain on.
>
> —Steve Jobs
> CEO, Apple Computer

GETTING CONNECTED

Check out the following web sites from the Professional Organizers Web Ring for helpful information about keeping your computer organized. Scroll down to find several helpful articles.

http://www.organizerswebring.com/poarticles/

WORKSHOP WRAP-UP

- A computer desktop will always have a few icons on it.
- Label computer files and documents so anyone can understand them.
- All computer documents should be saved in folders.
- Keep the current projects on your desktop.
- Clear out old files on your computer, but don't erase anything important.
- Save while you work, and periodically save work to disks.
- Use e-mail filters, e-mail file cabinets, and download folders to organize e-mail.
- A computer slowdown or crash is a sign that the computer is disorganized.
- You should run a defragmenting program periodically.